Cross-Country Ski Tours

of Washington's North Cascades

Tom Kirkendall & Vicky Spring

The Mountaineers • Seattle

THE MOUNTAINEERS: Organized 1906 "... to explore, study, preserve and enjoy the natural beauty of the Northwest."

3

5   4   3

Published by The Mountaineers
1011 S.W. Klickitat Way, Suite 107
Seattle, Washington 98134

Published simultaneously in Canada by Douglas & McIntyre, Ltd.
1615 Venables Street, Vancouver, British Columbia V5L 2H1

Edited by Andy Dappen
Copyedited by Nick Allison
Book layout by Ray Weisgerber
Cover designed by Judy Petry
Maps by Tom Kirkendall
Cover photo: Mt. Baker

Photos by the authors
Printed in the United States of America

Library of Congress Cataloging in Publication Data

Kirkendall, Tom.
   Cross-country ski tours of Washington's north Cascades / Tom
Kirkendall & Vicky Spring.
      p.   cm.
   Includes index.
   ISBN 0-89886-177-2 (pbk.) :
   1. Cross-country skiing—Cascade Range—Guide-books.   2. Cross
-country skiing—Washington (State)—Guide-books.   3. Cascade Range-
-Description and travel—Guide-books.   4. Washington (State)-
-Description and travel—1981- —Guide-books.   I. Spring, Vicky,
1953-   . II. Title.
GV854.5.C27K57   1988
917.97'5—dc19   88-8227
                                                        CIP

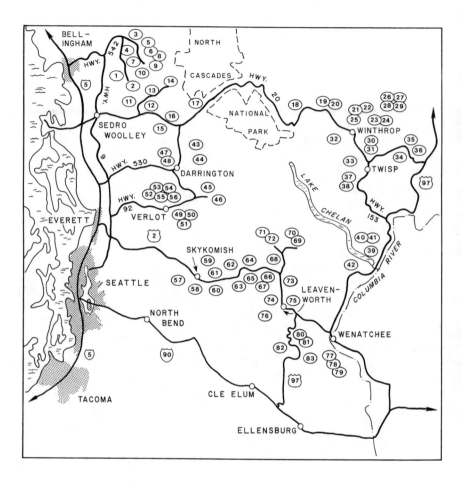

CONTENTS

PREFACE

WINTER WONDERLAND?

The Winter Wonderland—where has it gone? What ever happened to the vast quiet of snow time, the great peace beyond the racket of motors, the escape from machinery into a land where the fastest thing going was a rabbit?

Well, the ski mountaineer still can find it, but she may have to climb halfway up a cliff or to the top of a volcano to escape the racket of snowmobiles. As for the nordic skiers, we can learn to put up with the snarl of speeding snow machines—or we can start complaining to the Forest Service and the state parks department, demanding a fair share of the winter.

Let's face it, the snowmobile is a road gobbler. Nordic skiers traveling 2 to 3 miles an hour need only 6 to 12 miles of space for a day's recreation, and the only creatures that hear us are the local rabbits. A snowmobiler racing 30 to 100 miles an hour needs 50 to 100 miles of space for *his* day, and we can hear him counties away—a lucky thing, too, or you might not have time to duck.

Because snowmobilers are well organized and well financed by the industry and because they pay license fees and a gas tax, they can afford to buy friends in the state government and Forest Service. Snowmobile tax money helps to create jobs, groom trails, put up signs, and patrol the parking areas, giving the state and federal governments a vested interest in the industry and the sport.

To be fair, it must be said that the Forest Service would happily develop areas for cross-country skiing if somebody would pay them to do the job. However, nordic skiers are a poor bunch to look to for money. We grumble when we are forced to buy a Sno-Park permit and that little bit of money doesn't go very far.

Actually, the problem is not primarily financial. Nordic skiers don't need to be coddled. Groomed trails are nice, but most skiers are content with any old logging road. We merely ask that it be a *quiet* road and that snowmobiles not make it icy and rutted. The difficulty is that the very roads best suited for quiet gliding, especially by the beginning skier, are precisely those best for high-speed racketing.

Because snowmobilers have more money and make more noise (political, too), do they have the right to grab all the land they want? Skiers (and their quiet brethren, the snowshoers) constitute more than half the winter recreationist. Don't we deserve half of the winter? The money argument doesn't stand up; it wouldn't cost the Forest Service a fortune to nail up a few signs designating certain roads as solely for self-propelled sports and to mark these roads on the maps they hand out to snowmobilers for free.

Winter wonderland

There are endless possibilities in our winter wonderland.

Every time the Forest Service opens a road to snowmobiles, it should set aside an equally scenic road, of comparable length in the same area, for skiers and snowshoers.

The Forest Service knows in its heart what it *should* be doing. The Darrington Ranger District has designated three beautiful view roads for self-propelled sports in the South Fork Stillaguamish River Valley. But the *six* other roads in the same valley are for snowmobiles. (The self-propelled roads are so popular that on a winter weekend you may have to park a half mile away from the start of the tour, while there is plenty of spare parking at the snowmobile road-heads).

Some districts mark and even groom loops a mile or two long through the forest, but these efforts miss the point. Most people want to ski or snowshoe to a viewpoint, a lake, or some other scenic destination. Moreover, they want to do so free from the racket, stink, danger, and tracks of machines.

If nordic skiers ever expect to get justice, we're going to have to start making more noise—not in the wilderness, in the cities. We must repeatedly write letters to the Forest Service ranger districts and front headquarters as well as to the State Parks Office of Winter Recreation, requesting that a fair share of roads be returned to the Winter Wonderland. We must also join outdoor organizations, such as The Mountaineers, and work with them to put the same pressure on the Forest Service and the state parks department as is done by the snowmobile industry.

(90)	INTERSTATE FREEWAYS	(34)	SKI TOUR NUMBER
(2)	U.S. HIGHWAYS	✸	AVALANCHE HAZARD
(20)	STATE HIGHWAYS	⌂	LODGE
[69]	MAINLINE FOREST ROADS	⏢	HUT
[137]	SPUR FOREST ROADS		
	DRIVING ROADS		SKIING ROADS
	SKI LIFT		SKIING TRAILS

Mount Baker (Tour 9)

A NOTE ABOUT SAFETY

Cross-country skiing entails unavoidable risks, which every skier must assume. The listing of a route in this book does not guarantee it will be safe for anyone, at any time. Routes vary greatly in difficulty, and skiers vary greatly in skill and physical conditioning. Routes may have changed or conditions deteriorated since the descriptions were written. Also, conditions can change from day to day and even hour to hour, owing to weather and other factors.

Cross-country skiers can minimize the risks on a tour by being knowledgeable, prepared and alert. This book is not designed to fully prepare a skier for all problems encountered when skiing. Many good books are available on the subjects of wilderness survival, first aid, and equipment maintenance; consult one of them for information on these subjects.

It's important for all skiers to recognize their own limitations. Look ahead. If adverse conditions are stacking up against your skill and conditioning, abandon the trip.

INTRODUCTION

Every year more and more people head into the woods on nordic skis. Many are reformed downhillers fleeing from high prices, long lift lines, packed runs, and yodeling on the loudspeaker. Others are ski mountaineers seeking a less strenuous way to spend the winter. Some never have skied at all because neither of the other two forms of the sport appealed to them. Nordic, or cross-country, skiing is something completely different. Anyone can enjoy it—except, perhaps, people who absolutely despise snow.

Washington's Cascade and Olympic Mountains provide infinite opportunity for excellent nordic skiing, whether on groomed trails along peaceful valley floors, on scenic logging roads, or on open slopes of dormant volcanoes that cry out to be telemarked. This book can only begin to suggest how much there is to do and in how many areas. Particular emphasis has been given the needs of the beginning (basic) and intermediate skier who is just learning the country, but trails and routes have been included that will test the advanced and challenge the mountaineer.

To repeat the caution that any guidebook must offer—especially one that deals in so undependable a substance as snow—the reader must keep in mind the publication date of this book. If he skis onto the scene a couple of years later, he must understand that the authors have no control over (1) the building of new roads or washing out of old ones, (2) the rules and regulations of government agencies, and (3) the falling down of trees and the piling up (or not piling up) of snow. In a word: Conditions are never the same twice, so be flexible in your plans.

GUIDE TO THE GUIDEBOOK

User Designation

In order to help you choose a tour we have noted three different user classifications in the Appendix as follows:

Groomed Ski Trail: These are trails with machine-made tracks for skiers and are generally only found at resorts. There will be no machines, dogs, or avalanche dangers on these trails and you should expect to pay for their use.

Self-Propelled: These are areas closed to snowmobiles. You may have the company of snowshoers and hikers on your tour.

Multiple Use: These are tours on roads or trails that must be shared with snowmobiles and four-wheel drivers.

Skill Level

Each of the tours has been classified by the minimum skill required for an enjoyable trip. For the sake of simplicity we have used five levels that are broad and somewhat overlapping; consider them to be merely suggestions.

Basic: No skill requirement. Anyone can have fun the very first time on skis. These tours generally are in open meadows or valley bottoms, or on level logging roads.

Advanced Basic: The minimum skills required are good balance, kick-glide, and simple stopping techniques such as pole dragging, snowplow, and sitting down—and a good sense of humor. The tours at this level are generally on logging roads, marked Forest Service loops, or prepared tracks.

Intermediate: Tours at this level may be long, steep, or both. Intermediate-level skiers should have endurance and the ability to descend steep slopes in all types of snow conditions. Required skills include the kick-turn, herringbone, traverse, and snowplow turn. Tours at this level are generally on narrow, steep logging roads and may have optional off-road side trips and descent routes.

Advanced: The minimum skills at this level are full control of skis at all times, mastery of the telemark or any turn, and the ability to stop quickly. Some advanced tours require basic routefinding. Trails at this level include summer hiking trails and backcountry routes.

Mountaineer: The minimum skills required in addition to an advanced skill level are competence in routefinding and knowledge of snow and avalanche conditions, glacier travel, weather, winter camping, winter survival, and mountaineering.

Trip Length (X miles to a scenic place)

Snow levels vary from year to year and from day to day and therefore the starting point, especially on logging roads, may vary. A base point (which may or may not be your actual starting point) has been assigned; the trailhead elevation and skiing time are figured from this point.

Skiing Time

This is the time spent skiing to and from the destination and does not include lunch or rest stops. The times are calculated from the trail's base point. If the snowline is above this point, plan less time; if below, plan more. The times given for each trail assume good conditions. If a track must be broken through heavy snow or the surface is extremely hard ice, add a generous amount of extra time.

Variable Miles and Times

In some cases the number of miles and amount of skiing time given are variable. These trails are generally over logging roads where the snow level suggests different starting points and destinations in winter and spring.

Best Skiing Time

If you want to know what an "average" snow year is in Washington's Cascade or Olympic Mountains, don't ask a seasoned skier; all you'll get is a year-by-year description of the differences. There never is, in real life, an "average" winter. Some years skiing must be done at 5000 feet or above; other years skiing is good through June at 3000 feet; some years the skiing is superb on Seattle's golf courses for most of January.

In an attempt to say when skiing is best for each trail, certain generalizations have been made about that mythical average snow year. The time band given is a narrow one. Skiing often starts as much as a month before given times and lasts a month after. Some winters skiing may not be possible on trails below 4000 to 5000 feet. If in doubt, call the area ranger station, listen to pass reports, or contact local mountain shops before starting out.

Avalanche Potential

Tours in this book have been selected for their safety in winter and no known areas of extreme hazard have been included. The warnings given here are about areas to avoid at times when the snow is unstable. To know when these times are, skiers must make it their responsibility to inform themselves about current weather and snow conditions. The best source for up-to-date information on the weather and avalanche conditions in the Washington Cascades and Olympics is a weather radio with continuous reports from NOAA (National Oceanic and Atmospheric Administration). For specific tours call the ranger station in that district; on weekends there will be a recorded message.

Your best defense against avalanches is knowledge. Check "Suggested Reading" for detailed discussions. Several things to particularly watch for:

• Avalanche danger is especially high during *warming trends or after a heavy snowfall*; at these times avoid leeward slopes and travel on ridge tops.

• Steep hillsides, particularly north-facing, receive their first dose of sun for many months in the spring. After being stable all winter, these slopes may be covered by *spring,* or *climax, avalanches.*

• Wind causes snow to build up on the leeward side of ridges, creating dangerous overhangs called *cornices.* Use caution when approaching a ridge top—you may walk out atop a cornice with empty air beneath. A good rule is never to ski beyond the line of trees or snowblown rocks that mark the true crest of a ridge. It is equally dangerous to ski under a cornice as over it. Cornices may beak off and trigger avalanches below.

Forecasting agencies express the daily hazard in the following four classifications:

1. Low Avalanche Hazard—mostly stable snow.
2. Moderate Avalanche Hazard—areas of unstable snow on steep, open slopes or gullies.

3. High Avalanche Hazard—snow pack very unstable. Avalanches highly probable on steep slopes and in gullies.
4. Extreme Avalanche Hazard—travel in the mountains unsafe. Better to head for the beach.

These classifications of *hazard* have to do with the *weather's* contribution to the avalanches. Each trail in this book has been rated as to the *potential* of the *terrain* for avalanches. The two factors of hazard and potential must be put together by the skier to make an accurate judgment of the situation.

If the avalanche potential for the trail is listed as *none,* the trail may be safely skied on days when the hazard is low, moderate, or high.

Areas with *low* avalanche potential normally may be skied on days when the hazard is low or moderate.

A *moderate* avalanche potential indicates the area is always to be skied with caution and then only when the hazard is low.

Avalanche forecasting is not an exact science. As when driving a car, one has to accept a certain amount of risk and use the forecast as a guide, not as a certainty. It is important always to seek up-to-date avalanche information before each trip even for trips of low to moderate avalanche potential.

Maps

Blankets of snow add new difficulties to routefinding. Signs are covered, road junctions are obscured, and trails blend into the surrounding countryside. Never start out without a good map of the area to be skied.

To help you find the best map for your tour, we have recommended a topographic map (USGS, Green Trails or both) in the description of each trip. The USGS maps are published by the U.S. Geological Survey. These maps cover the entire country and are unequaled for off-road and off-trail routefinding. Unfortunately, USGS maps are not kept up-to-date in terms of roads and trails. The Green Trails maps are published in Washington and regularly updated; however, these maps do not cover areas beyond the heartland of the Cascades and Olympics.

Both the USGS and Green Trails maps are available at outdoor equipment stores and many Forest Service ranger stations. Another excellent resource is an up-to-date Forest Service Recreation Map, available for a small fee at ranger stations (weekdays) or by writing the district offices.

Sno-Parks

Sno-Parks are designated winter parking areas plowed throughout the winter for recreationists. Permits are required to park in these areas and the fees provide funds to keep the parking sites open. Cars parking without permits can count on a ticket and possible towing.

Permits are available at outdoor equipment stores or by mail from:
Office of Winter Recreation
Washington State Parks and Recreation Commission
7150 Cleanwater Lane KY-11
Olympia, Washington 98505   Phone: (206) 754-1250

Snow-Play Areas

As the name suggests, these are areas to enjoy the snow by walking, sledding, snowshoeing, skiing, or any other nonmotorized activity. They are great for families and are usually located only a short way from the car. A few require a Sno-Park permit, but most are plowed out by the Forest Service. For specific location contact a ranger station.

HEADING OUT INTO WINTER

This book doesn't explain *how* to ski, just *where*. However, some tips are offered to help orient skiers toward wintertime fun. Further information can be found in "Suggested Reading."

Technique

Cross-country (or nordic) skiing looks simple enough, but proper technique is very important to ensure a good time. Even expert downhillers have problems the first day on nordic skis. The narrowness, flexible bindings, and low shoes give an entirely different feeling. Books are helpful, but one or two lessons may be needed. Many organizations offer a two-lesson plan, the first to get you started in the right direction and the second to correct any problems you have.

Clothing

There is no dress code for cross-country skiing. Clothing can be anything from high-fashion Lycra® to mismatched army surplus. However, many of the garments sold for cross-country skiing are designed for resort skiing or racing, providing flexibility and style, but not much warmth.

In the wilderness, warmth is crucial. Covering your body from head to toe in wool or polypropylene, using two or more layers on the upper body to regulate heating, ensures a pleasant journey rather than a bone-chilling ordeal. So go ahead and wear that designer outfit, but be sure and have a layer of long underwear on underneath and another layer with you that can be put on over it.

Rain gear is essential. A poncho keeps snow and rain off of a person who is standing still, but can be somewhat awkward when one is skiing. Rain pants and jackets made of coated nylon or breathable waterproof material work best for warmth, dryness, and flexibility.

Skis and Boots

What length of ski to buy, with side cut or without, with metal edges or without, hard or soft camber? What boots are best, high- or low-topped? These and many more questions could fill a book—and they do. Our one and only suggestion is to purchase a waxless ski as your first pair. Learning to ski can be complicated enough without the frustration of trying to wax for the ever-changing snow conditions. When looking for that new pair of skis, avoid stores that just happen to have a few cross-country skis in stock. Stores that have special cross-country departments and employees who enjoy cross-country skiing will be able to give you a better understanding of what you need and what you don't.

Cross-country boots come in two varieties, lightweight and flexible for track skiing and light touring, and heavyweight with lug soles for backcountry and telemark skiing. The type of boots you have will determine the type of bindings you need, so buy the boots first.

What to Take

Every skier who ventures into the wilderness should be prepared to spend the night out. Winter storms can come with great speed and force, creating whiteouts that leave the skier with nowhere to go. Each ski pack must include the ten essentials, plus one:

1. Extra clothing—more than needed in the worst of weather.
2. Extra food—there should be some left over at the end of the trip.
3. Sunglasses—a few hours of bright sun on snow can cause a pounding headache or temporary blindness.
4. Knife—for first aid and emergency repairs.
5. First-aid kit—just in case.
6. Fire starter—chemical starter to get wet wood burning.
7. Matches in a waterproof container—to start a fire.
8. Flashlight—be sure to have extra batteries with bulb.
9. Map—make sure it's the right one for the trip.
10. Compass—keep in mind the declination.

Plus 1: Repair kit—including a spare ski tip, spare screws and binding bail (if changeable), heavy-duty tape, a few feet of braided picture wire and heavy string, and a combination wrench-pliers-screwdriver.

Other items to carry may include a small shovel, sun cream, and a large plastic tarp to use as a "picnic blanket" or for emergency shelter. All these items should fit comfortably into a day pack. Obviously, a fanny pack will not hold all the items listed above. Fanny packs are strictly for track and resort skiing where one is carrying only a sandwich and a few waxes.

Winter Camping

Most campgrounds are closed in winter by snow. However, some state parks remain open with plowed access roads and one or two campsites and offering the added attraction of heated restrooms.

When winter camping takes you out into wilderness, camp wherever you feel safe. Avoid pitching a tent under trees heavy with snow; when least expected (day or night), "mushrooms" may fall from above and crush your tent.

Whether in the backcountry or on groomed tracks of a resort, carry out your garbage. (If you packed it in full, you can pack it out empty.) Burying leftovers under a few inches of snow only hides them until the spring melt. Also be careful with human waste. Hidden beneath the snow may be a stream or a summer hiking trail.

Water can be difficult to come by in winter. Most small streams are either hidden beneath the snow or flowing in grand white canyons too steep to descend. If day-skiing, carry water. On a trip lasting overnight or longer, carry a long string for lowering a bucket to an open stream as well as a stove and enough fuel to melt snow. Even in winter, the water from streams in areas where people and/or beavers and other such critters live in summer should be boiled or chemically purified.

When spending the day or several days out skiing, take care where you park your car. A sudden winter storm can make bare and dry logging roads deep in white and impossible to drive, leaving your car stranded— maybe until the spring melt. Always travel with a shovel in the car and a watchful eye on the weather.

Pets

Although in some jurisdictions the family pet is permitted to tag along on summer hikes, wintertime should be left to the two-legged family members. Skiing through knee-deep powder is lots of fun, but not for the ski-less family pet, floundering in a white morass. Pets also tend to destroy ski tracks by leaving behind deep paw prints and brown klister.

Multiple-Use

Until more areas can be designated skier-only, sharing the way with snowshoers, snowmobilers, dog sleds, and four-wheel drivers will have to be tolerated. However, multiple-use is not totally impossible. For example, in the Methow Valley snowmobilers and skiers understand and respect each other's rights and needs. The snowmobilers know the difference between their machines, which destroy ski trails, and the mechanical ski-tracking machines, which create grooves for skis. In exchange for the snowmobilers' courtesy, skiers make their tracks on the edge of a road, leaving the middle for the speeding machines.

Be Flexible

During research for this book many ranger districts and ski patrols were interviewed and one point was stressed: "Be flexible." Have an alternate, safer trip plan if weather changes to create a high avalanche potential in your favorite area. If your second choice is also unsafe, plan a walk along a beach or to the city park. Your exercise of good judgment will help ranger districts and ski areas avoid the necessity of total winter closure for *all* users in order to protect a few thoughtless ones from their own stupidity.

1 GLACIER CREEK

Lookout Mountain

Skill level: basic
Round trip: 10 miles
Skiing time: 5 hours
Elevation gain: 2000 feet
High point: 4500 feet
Best: December and March–
*   mid-April*
Avalanche potential: low
Map: Green Trails, Mount Baker

Mount Baker Vista

Skill level: advanced basic
Round trip: 8 miles
Skiing time: 4 hours
Elevation gain: 2500 feet
High point: 5000 feet
Best: December and March–
*   mid-April*
Avalanche potential: moderate
Map: Green Trails, Mount Baker

Unbeatable views and easy terrain make tours up Lookout Mountain and Mount Baker Vista enjoyable in early or late season. Furthermore, these tours follow logging roads that are fun for track and skate skiers and have off-road potential to attract telemark and backcountry explorers.

Snow-covered trees near Lookout Mountain

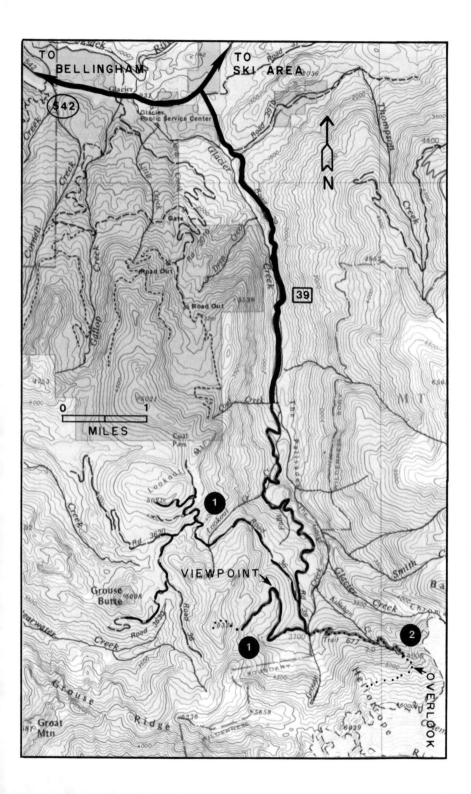

Expect to encounter snowmobiles on this tour all winter long. Early in the season the numbers are not overwhelming, but by midwinter the going gets ugly—Glacier Creek Road is groomed for snowmobiles. Ski here before Christmas or after mid-March, when the road can be driven to an elevation of 2500 to 3000 feet. If in doubt call the Forest Service Information Center in Glacier before leaving home.

Access: Drive the Mount Baker Highway, State Route 542, to the town of Glacier. Pass the Forest Service Information Center at the east end of town and continue east .6 mile before turning right on Glacier Creek road No. 39. Head up the valley on the narrow, paved road until blocked by snow. When conditions are best, the road should be open between Coal Creek at the 5-mile mark and Lookout Creek near the 6-mile mark.

Lookout Mountain: The Glacier Creek Road climbs steadily above Coal Creek through second-growth forest with few views until clearcuts are reached 2 miles above Coal Creek. The road divides 2½ miles from Coal Creek (3500 feet). Before turning right on Road 36, feast your eyes on the towering walls of Chowder Ridge, the rounded dome of Hadley Peak, the Roosevelt and Coleman glaciers tumbling off Mount Baker, and the dark profile of the Black Buttes hovering above Heliotrope and Grouse ridges.

For the next 2 miles, Road 36 heads back into the Lookout Creek drainage, climbing gently with views of snow-plastered Church Mountain. After crossing Lookout Creek at 3900 feet, the road reaches an intersection 4½ miles from Coal Creek. Options abound. Skiers wishing to avoid more climbing should stay to the left on Road 36 and left again ½ mile beyond to reach a broad, level valley below Grouse Butte. Skiers opting for the best views should turn right at 4½ miles on Road 36 and head up Lookout Mountain. Stay right at the first intersection. At the second intersection the left fork leads to the 5021-foot summit of Lookout Mountain, while the right fork contours to a saddle just north of the summit. You'll find excellent skiing in the clearcuts located on all sides of Lookout Mountain.

Mount Baker Vista: From the Road 36 turnoff, 2½ miles above Coal Creek, continue straight ahead on Road 39. The road reaches the Mount Baker Vista, a viewpoint worthy of a long rest at 4700 feet, 4 miles above Coal Creek.

If time and energy allow, continue up the road to its end at 5000 feet and then ski west to the summit of a 5328-foot hill. The snowmobiles head to the open meadows, and skiers who hide their pride and follow the machine tracks will find secluded bowls for telemarking on the flanks of Grouse Ridge. Exercise caution here. The steeper hillsides will slide after a heavy snowfall and on warm days in the spring.

2 HELIOTROPE RIDGE

Skill level: advanced
Round trip: 13 miles to Coleman
  Glacier viewpoint
Skiing time: 1–2 days
Elevation gain: 3700 feet
High point: 6500 feet
Best: October–November,
  April–mid-June
Avalanche potential: low
Map: Green Trails, Mount Baker

See map on page 23.

On Heliotrope Ridge

From a camp near the edge of crevasse-slashed and icefall-tumbled Coleman Glacier, set winding ski tracks through secluded bowls and across steep slopes of Heliotrope Ridge. In the evening return to the doorstep of the tent and watch one of nature's best shows, a brief and brilliant winter sunset casting pinks and golds over snowy ramparts of Mount Baker—or maybe crawl in the tent and peer out at a blizzard.

The route to the northwest side of Mount Baker culminates in 3 miles of trail, but starts with 10 miles of road, some or all of which may have to be skied. Because the road is extremely popular with four-wheelers and machine skiers, cross-country skiers are advised to do this trip in fall or spring when the road is partially or totally free of snow and gas-powered travelers. A special warning about late fall: The possibility of a car's being snowed in for the winter is very real. If 6 inches of snow pile up, that is the time to leave—or be already gone.

Access: Drive Highway 542 to Glacier and register your trip at the Forest Service Information Center at the east end of town. At .6 mile past the Information Center turn right on Glacier Creek Road and follow it to the snowline or trailhead. At 5 miles the road bumps over Coal Creek and starts serious climbing. This generally marks the beginning of spring skiing (around 2000 feet).

The Tour: The road climbs by occasional views of Coleman Glacier and its headwall on the glacier-torn face of Mount Baker. At a large junction at 2¾ miles take a left fork ¼ mile to the trailhead parking lot (3700 feet).

Descend left into heavy timber to find the trail, generally discernible all winter. Skiers with skins will probably wish to use them on the steep trail. Many find it preferable to walk.

Mount Baker from the Coleman Glacier overlook

At 2 miles, just below timberline (4700 feet), is the site of Kulshan Cabin, torn down in 1986. Continue on 1 more mile to excellent campsites in scraggly trees 500 feet west of the Coleman Glacier overlook.

The best skiing lies west of the camp area, separated from it by a series of steep, slide-prone gullies. Ski up open slopes from the glacier overlook, bearing right. When the terrain levels into a broad bench at about 6500 feet, turn right and head over rolling Heliotrope Ridge and drop down steep slopes to the bowls beyond.

Many skiers find the long open slopes leading to the summit of Mount Baker extremely alluring. However, the attempt must not be made without climbing gear as deep crevasses lie under the smooth snow.

3 CANYON CREEK

Skill level: intermediate
Round trip: 4–10 miles
Skiing time: 2–6 hours
Elevation gain: up to 3000 feet

High point: 5699 feet on Excelsior
  Peak
Best: mid-March–May
Avalanche potential: low
Map: Green Trails, Mount Baker

Throughout the winter Canyon Creek Road and its many offshoots are a popular haunt of snowmobilers. However, when the spring sun starts shining and the racketeers set their snow machines aside, skiers are free to explore four areas out of Canyon Creek drainage.

Access: Drive Highway 542 east to Glacier and 2 miles beyond. Turn left on Canyon Creek road No. 31 and go to your choice of the options below.

Kidney Creek Road: Drive Road 31 for 7.5 miles, then go right on Road 3130 (2150 feet), and drive to the snowline. The Kidney Creek Road climbs steadily up a steep hillside, through clearcuts and forest, to an intersection at 6½ miles (4900 feet). Here the left spur goes ½ mile north along the ridge top to views over Canyon Creek to Bald Mountain and the British Columbia Coast Range. The right fork follows the ridge top south for another mile. Advanced skiers may continue on beyond the road to open meadows below Church Mountain.

Shoulder of Church Mountain from the Kidney Creek Road

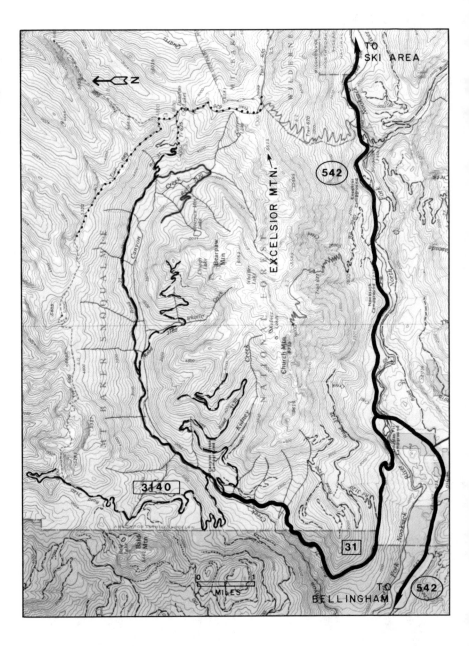

Bald Mountain Road: Drive the Canyon Creek Road 8 miles from Highway 542. Cross Canyon Creek, then go left on Road 3140 (2200 feet). Follow the road 5 miles, skirting Bald Mountain, then leave the road and ski clearcuts to an open ridge top and peer over into Canada barely 1½ miles away.

Whistler Creek Road: Follow Canyon Creek Road 10 miles from Highway 542, then take a right onto Road 3160 (2600 feet). Cross Canyon Creek and follow Whistler Creek 1½ miles before starting the serious climb 2½ miles to a ridge top at 4900 feet, below Bearpaw Mountain.

Excelsior Mountain Trail: (recommended for advanced or mountaineer skiers). For the greatest of late, late spring skiing to spectacular views and open slopes, drive Road 31 for 15 miles from Highway 542 to the Excelsior Mountain Trailhead (4200 feet). The trail climbs through timber, gaining 300 feet in the first ¾ mile to meet the Canyon Ridge Trail. Go right, passing to the east of the Damfino Lakes (4500 feet). Ski the next mile up through forest, then climb a gully to reach meadows at 5100 feet, 2½ miles from the road. To the south is a spectacular view of Mounts Baker and Shuksan. To the north is British Columbia, dotted with the white-topped Border Peaks and the glacier-coated Coast Range. Plan to spend at least one entire day telemarking on the long, rolling snow-covered meadows.

NOOKSACK RIVER

4 WELLS CREEK

Winter Viewpoint

Skill level: intermediate
Round trip: 6 miles
Skiing time: 4 hours
Elevation gain: 1100 feet
High point: 2600 feet
Best: mid-December–February
Avalanche potential: none
Map: Green Trails, Mount Baker

Cougar Divide

Skill level: intermediate
Round trip: up to 16 miles
Skiing time: 1–2 days
Elevation gain: 2400 feet
High point: 4900 feet
Best: April–May
Avalanche potential: high in
* midwinter*
Map: Green Trails, Mount Baker

In winter there is a high overlook of the Nooksack River with views from Church Mountain east to the glaciered peaks of Mount Sefrit and Ruth Mountain crowning the Nooksack Ridge. In spring, as the snow melts back to allow vehicle access up Wells Creek Road, there is the long Cougar Divide leading to the undisputed lord of the area, Mount Baker.

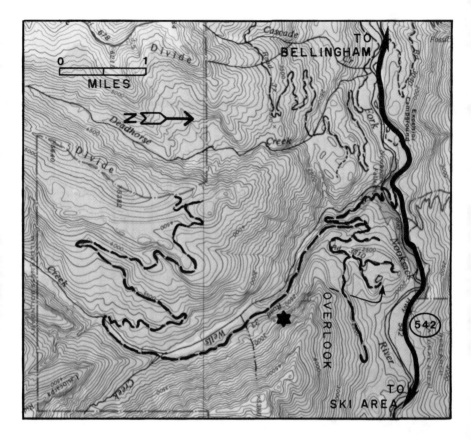

Access: Drive Highway 542 east beyond the Glacier Ranger Station 6.8 miles. A small parking area usually is plowed at the Wells Creek turnoff (1700 feet).

The Tour: The winter trip starts by descending the first ½ mile to cross the Nooksack River (1500 feet), just above Nooksack Falls. (The falls trail is steep, icy, and best left for summer visits.) Beyond the river the road climbs slowly but steadily through winter-stilled forest. Just past the 2-mile marker the road forks (2000 feet). Winter skiers go left, climbing a steep road through logging clearings, noticeably messy even in winter. In 200 yards turn right and head around the edge of the clearcut at an unmarked intersection. The road climbs through young timber plantations until splitting again at 2¾ miles. The right fork wanders on another 1½ miles, heading gently downhill. The left fork climbs steeply to a flat-topped knoll with wide views. Roam the whole knoll for views from each direction. However, stay well back from the edges if not equipped with a parachute—there are cliffs with overhangs and snow cornices to the north, west, and south.

For the spring trip drive to the snowline. Be sure conditions have stabilized before setting out; open slopes below Barometer Mountain between miles 3 and 5 have a high avalanche potential after a heavy snow. At 5 miles the road leaves Wells Creek and follows Bar Creek a mile, then begins a long climb towards Cougar Divide. The road divides at the ridge top. The right fork climbs north ½ mile to an overlook of Wells Creek, 5770-foot Barometer Mountain, and Mount Baker. The left fork heads south ½ mile along the divide. Mountaineer skiers may ski 2 more miles along the rolling crest toward the awesomely glaciered mass of Mount Baker.

Mount Sefrit from the overlook

5 TWIN LAKES ROAD

Skill level: advanced basic
Round trip: 8 miles
Skiing time: 4 hours
Elevation gain: 1900 feet

High point: 3900 feet
Best: mid-December–March
Avalanche potential: low
Map: Green Trails, Mount Shuksan

Although it is too dangerous to ski all the way to Twin Lakes, the "safe" section of the road is an excellent winter tour, starting in the rain forest and climbing briskly up to a steep, narrow valley. The high point of the tour is the rapid descent, equally suited for bobsleds as for skis.

Access: Drive Highway 542 east 12.5 miles from Glacier. Pass the Department of Highways work sheds and the Twin Lakes Road turnoff. Drive on .2 mile and turn left at the Hannegan Road (see Tour 6). Park here (2200 feet).

The Tour: Walk back along Mount Baker Highway .2 mile to the Twin Lakes Road and head up. The road starts climbing immediately up the forested hillside. Mile 1 is marked by a small bench followed by more climbing that shows renewed vigor, on the part of the road at least. Pass several spur roads. When in doubt about which road is which, stay left.

Shortly after mile 2 pass Keep Kool Trail, marking the road's entrance to a narrow valley boxed in by Yellow Aster Butte to the west and Goat Mountain to the east. Here the road levels, traversing open slopes above Swamp Creek for nearly ½ mile. Just as the road is about to plunge back into forest comes an important junction. This time, *take the right fork,*

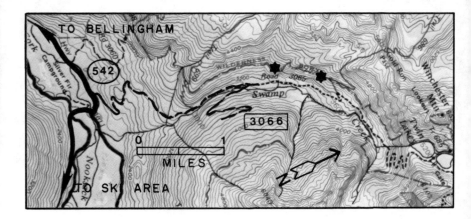

Twin Lakes Road

spur road 3066. (If you follow the Twin Lakes Road to its natural end you may come to an unnatural end in a thundering avalanche.)

Spur road 3066 descends briefly to cross Swamp Creek (3100 feet), then switchbacks rapidly up through new-growth forest to its end at 4 miles (3900 feet) and views of Yellow Aster Butte.

6 NORTH FORK NOOKSACK

Skill level: basic
Round trip: 2–10 miles
Skiing time: 2–6 hours
Elevation gain: 400 feet

High point: 2600 feet
Best: January–mid-March
Avalanche potential: low
Map: Green Trails, Mount Shuksan

It is unclear whether skiers are drawn to this road primarily by the nearly level terrain, the outstanding scenery, or the closure to snowmobiles. Whatever the reason, the North Fork Nooksack River Road is a popular tour for novices and experts alike.

Access: Drive Highway 542 east from Glacier 12.5 miles. Just before the highway crosses the North Fork (2200 feet), the Hannegan Road, the start of the route, goes off left. Park in the small parking space provided.

The Tour: The Hannegan Road follows the North Fork Nooksack River upstream along the valley floor, open and level. Views start immediately, Mount Shuksan gleaming in winter white, Mount Sefrit and Ruth Mountain standing out along Nooksack Ridge.

At ½ mile cross a clearing to open forest. Several spur roads branch off in this area; stay left at all junctions. At 1½ miles the road splits. Hannegan Road goes left up Ruth Creek 4 miles to the road-end at Hannegan Campground, the whole way in dense forest with few views after the first mile. Avalanche hazard is high after the first mile and winter travel is not recommended. From the split, the North Fork Nooksack River road No.

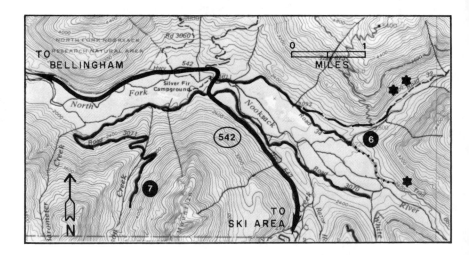

34 goes right, skirting the north side of the valley. At 3 miles ridges close in and the valley narrows; this is a good turnaround point when the snow is unstable.

The final 2 miles climb 300 feet to the start of the Nooksack Cirque Trail, not recommended for winter travel because of very high avalanche hazard.

Mount Shuksan and the North Fork of the Nooksack River

7 SILVER FIR

Anderson Creek

Skill level: advanced basic
Round trip: 10 miles
Skiing time: 5 hours
Elevation gain: 1200 feet
High point: 3400 feet
Best: mid-December–mid-March
Avalanche potential: low
Map: Green Trails, Mount
   Shuksan

Nooksack River

Skill level: basic
Round trip: 8 miles
Skiing time: 4 hours
Elevation gain: none
High point: 2240 feet
Best: mid-December–mid-March
Avalanche potential: none
Map: Green Trails, Mount
   Shuksan

See map on page 34.

The area around Silver Fir Campground has been developed by the Salmon Ridge Ski Touring Company as a cross-country skiing center and boasts 25 kilometers of groomed trails. In 1987, after a couple of poor snow years, the company owners were looking for a higher location for their trails and most likely will have relocated to the White Salmon Road (see Tour 8) by the winter of 1988 or 1989.

Whether the area is tracked or untracked, good skiing exists on either side of Highway 542. On the south side, Anderson Creek Road offers a two-part trip. The first part follows a long, gentle descent along the open swamplands of the Nooksack River's north fork. The second part is a steady climb into the hanging valley of Anderson Creek, left high above the Nooksack when glaciers carved out that river valley.

On the north side of Highway 542, Road 3070 parallels the Nooksack River past swamps and forests to the road's end at White Salmon Creek.

Access: Drive Highway 542 east from Glacier 12.8 miles. Five hundred feet after crossing the North Fork Nooksack River, turn left into the Salmon Ridge parking lot or, if the touring company has moved, right to a small plowed-out area on the side of the highway. If the area is being groomed, a trail fee must be paid on weekends and holidays at the warming hut (2200 feet).

Anderson Creek: The Anderson Creek tour starts on the south side of the highway, following Road 3071 west. (Do not confuse this road with the entrance to the Silver Fir Campground just to the right.) The first 2½ miles run gently downhill and go quickly, especially if the road has been freshly groomed. The road crosses Anderson Creek for the first time near mile 1. Just before the 2-mile marker the road begins to climb, and at 2½ miles is an intersection which, in 1987, marked the end of the groomed trail (2200 feet).

Anderson Creek Road and the North Fork of the Nooksack River Valley

Follow the main road to the left as it starts to climb. Look for the occasional view of Yellow Aster Butte and Goat Mountain across the valley. Near mile 4 the scene changes as the road crosses Anderson Creek again (3000 feet), makes a steep switchback, and enters the creek's hanging valley. To the west, the steep sides of Barometer Mountain offer a formidable barrier while Slate Mountain boxes you in on the east.

The road ends in a clearcut just after the 5-mile marker at the Anderson Creek trailhead, a trail that goes on up the valley another mile to nowhere in particular. The ski back down the road to the valley is quick, but remember to pace yourself for the final level stretch along the Nooksack River.

Nooksack River: Road 3070 starts at the far side of the open clearing, heading east to the Nooksack River where it turns southeast. The road climbs away from the river at 1½ miles and descends back to the valley floor at 2½ miles to cross Bagley Creek. The road ends after 4 miles at White Salmon Creek. If the Salmon Ridge Touring Company is still grooming the area, try one of the alternate trails for the return journey.

8 WHITE SALMON CREEK

Skill level: basic
Round trip: 5 miles
Skiing time: 2 hours
Elevation gain: 320 feet

High point: 3840 feet
Best: December–mid-April
Avalanche potential: none
Map: Green Trails, Mount Stuart

Three words best describe the tour along White Salmon Creek: fun, easy, scenic. The trip follows logging roads and clearcuts to the lower slopes of Shuksan Arm, located on the edge of the Mount Baker Wilderness, and offers a front-seat view of glaciers and cliffs rising directly to the summit of Mount Shuksan.

The fate of this tour is not entirely clear. In 1987 skiing and parking were free. In future years, however, the area may have groomed cross-

Sunset on Mount Shuksan

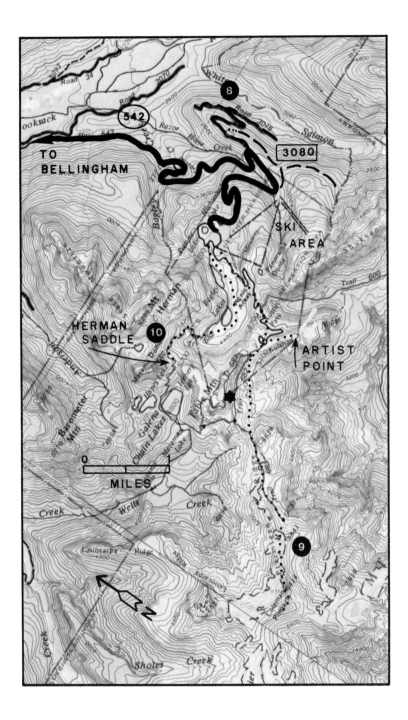

country trails and fees will be charged to ski here on weekends and holidays. Contact the Forest Service Information Center in Glacier for up-to-date information.

Access: Drive the Mount Baker Highway, State Route 542, east 18.6 miles from the town of Glacier to Forest Road 3075, where a plowed parking area marks the start of the tour (3520 feet).

The Tour: Views pop up immediately as the road makes a short climb, then levels off to contour north. Across the Nooksack River Valley, Tomyhoi and Yellow Aster Butte are the first peaks visible. After ¾ mile the road bends back south around the end of a ridge and begins descending. Leave the road here and ski up through a clearcut, following the ridge while gaining 150 feet of elevation, to meet Road 3080.

Road 3080 continues to follow the ridge line for ½ mile to a broad logging platform. Stay left to ski around the base of a clearcut hill and a ski run from the Mount Baker Area, then head back into the forest. The road ends at 2½ miles at the top of a logged clearing, overlooking White Salmon Creek and yielding a magnifying-glass view of Mount Shuksan. From your vantage point, you overlook the sheer rock walls and steep glaciers that rise straight up to the summit. In the spring, thundering avalanches can sometimes be seen crashing down the face.

NOOKSACK RIVER

9 ARTIST POINT AND COLEMAN PINNACLE

Artist Point

Skill level: intermediate
Round trip: 5 miles
Skiing time: 3 hours
Elevation gain: 1100 feet
High point: 5220 feet
Best: December–May
Avalanche potential: low
Maps: Green Trails, Mount Shuksan; USGS, Mount Shuksan

Coleman Pinnacle

Skill level: mountaineer
Round trip: 11 miles
Skiing time: 6 hours
Elevation gain: 2080 feet
High point: 6200 feet
Best: December–May
Avalanche potential: high
Maps: Green Trails, Mount Shuksan; USGS, Mount Shuksan

See map on page 39.

No one who visits Artist Point on a clear day can question the name of the place, located between the vertical massif of Mount Shuksan and the (restlessly?) slumbering dome of Mount Baker. The scene is further embellished by hardy trees plastered with wind-driven snow like so many lonesome statues.

Mount Baker from Kulshan Ridge

Coleman Pinnacle a sharp spike in the long spine of Ptarmigan Ridge, situated between Artist Point and Mount Baker. The pinnacle reigns over excellent powder bowls and runs that are over 1000 vertical feet long. The tour out to the pinnacle is highly avalanche-prone and is unsafe unless the snow is quite stable. Be sure and talk with the Forest Service snow ranger before heading out.

Access: Driver Highway 542 east from Bellingham 55 miles to its end at the Mount Baker Ski Area (4120 feet). (On Mondays and Tuesdays the road to the ski area is not plowed.) Park with the downhill skiers and head out. There has been some attempt by the ski area to collect a parking fee from cross-country skiers. The owners can charge a fee for parking in their lot, but they cannot charge for parking along the road. Parking by the warming hut and around Picture Lake is free.

Artist Point: From the south end of the upper parking lot ski along the edge of the ski area, following the summer road to Austin Pass. Stay out of the path of the downhillers. (You may pass by the fee box, set out for cross-country skiers using their cat tracks, with a clear conscience; you are heading far beyond the limits of the ski area.)

Ski below the rope tow, then up the steep hill at the ski-area boundary. Here folks with climbing skins will zip by their herringboning and kick-

Mount Shuksan from Artist Point

turning comrades. At Austin Pass (4700 feet), bear right. Skiers with climbing skins can take the quick route, straight up the next hill. Others will contour on the road east to gentler slopes, then climb over rolling terrain to the crest of Kulshan Ridge (4900 feet). Be wary of the drop-off on the far side—don't let enthusiasm for the view draw you beyond the trees that mark the brink.

To the right along the ridge are imposing cliffs of Table Mountain, so turn left along Kulshan Ridge to Artist Point, 200 feet higher and ¼ mile farther. Be sure to bring a big lunch because once on Artist Point the hours disappear as in a dream amid the breathtaking beauty.

Coleman Pinnacle: There are two approaches. The shortest is to ski to Kulshan Ridge (see above). On the ridge climb to the right. Near the base of Table Mountain drop over the ridge and descend 200 vertical feet down the steep south side of the ridge, then traverse along the lower edge of the steep slope of Table Mountain to a 5000-foot saddle. This is an area of extreme avalanche danger. Do not attempt to cross below Table Mountain when the snow pack is unstable.

The alternate approach is via Herman Saddle (see Tour 10) and Chain Lakes. This route has some extra climbing and is longer. If the day is a warm one, use this as your return route.

Once beyond Table Mountain, climb up Ptarmigan Ridge and ski along the ridge tops, staying as much as possible on the southeast side. The pinnacle is an obvious rocky spur and the fourth major high point encountered along the ridge. Ski around the pinnacle to the east side then head down the bowl on the west side. Snow remains light here for much of the season and the run is outstanding.

The return may be made by skiing well west from the steep slopes of Ptarmigan Ridge and making a short climb back to the 5000-foot pass south of Table Mountain.

10 HERMAN SADDLE

Skill level: advanced
Round trip: 5 miles
Skiing time: 4–6 hours
Elevation gain: 1060 feet
High point: 5300 feet
Best: December–June

Avalanche potential: moderate
Maps: Green Trails, Mount
Shuksan; USGS, Mount
Shuksan

See map on page 39.

The Herman Saddle tour offers some of the finest downhill cross-country skiing in the western Cascades, on snow that is frequently powdery and light, down an open bowl smoother than most groomed slopes. Views of Mount Shuksan and Mount Baker are huge beyond Table Moun-

Skiers descending the open slopes below Herman Saddle

tain and other foreground peaks—and the entire tour is in plain view of
lift skiers on Panorama Dome.

Note: Avalanches are very common on the route, which should not be
attempted after a heavy snowfall or in warming spells. In addition, the
route is easily lost in times of poor visibility. Always consult the ranger
before setting out.

Access: Drive to the Mount Baker Ski Area parking lot (4120 feet). Begin
as for Artist Point (see Tour 9).

The Tour: At the Austin Pass rope tow, drop to the old warming hut,
then go left along a bench to its end. Descend to the white plain below,
where the two Bagley Lakes lie hidden under a blanket of snow. See how
avalanches have swept across this little basin and contemplate the fool-
hardiness of skiing here during periods of instability.

Cross the basin and head for Herman Saddle, the lowest and most obvious pass in the circle of peaks between Table Mountain and Mazama
Dome. As the basin bends west, the ascent begins. Skiers with climbing
skins will be glad; for those without, there commences a long series of
switchbacks to gain the next 800 feet. Stay to the right side of the basin on
the flanks of Mount Herman, well away from the basin headwall. Near
the top, at around 5100 feet, head left (south), contouring below Mazama
Dome to reach the saddle at 5300 feet. On the way up plan your descent.
Decide which slopes you want to mark with graceful figure-eights (or
sitzmarks) for lift skiers on Panorama Dome to admire and envy (or
laugh at).

Camp Robbers impatiently waiting for a hand-out

11 PARK BUTTE

Skill level: advanced
Round trip: 18 miles
Skiing time: 1–3 days
Elevation gain: 3100 feet
High point: 5000 feet
Best: March–May
Avalanche potential: moderate
Maps: Green Trails, Lake Shannon
*   and Hamilton*

Cross-country ski trail sign

A single day, no matter how long, is not enough for Park Butte and the adjoining flanks of Mount Baker. Carry camping gear to ensure sufficient time to tour snow-covered meadows, then climb a hill to view the Black Buttes and Twin Sisters, and watch steam rise from the volcano's crater.

Sad to say, the wide-open spaces attract snow machines like a picnic does ants. Until the Forest Service recognizes that this spectacular area is the wrong place for "racketeers," skiers will be happier if they visit late in the season or on a weekday.

Access: Drive Highway 20 east from Sedro Woolley 14.5 miles and go left on Baker Lake Road. At 12.5 miles, just after crossing Rocky Creek, turn left on Loomis-Nooksack road No. 12. In midwinter this is the starting point. In spring the road usually is open another 3.5 miles to the junction of Loomis-Nooksack Road and Schreibers Meadow road No. 13 (1900 feet).

The Tour: Ski the right fork, Road 13. At ½ mile a spur branches off to Dillard Point; stay left. Climb to a second spur road at 1½ miles (2700 feet); again stay left. At 2 miles the road levels and the next 3 miles up the valley are nearly flat. At 5 miles go left off Road 13 on a well-signed, heavily traveled snowmobile track. Follow orange markers across Sulphur Creek on a wooden bridge and ½ mile to Schreibers Meadow (3263 feet).

Turn right along Sulphur Creek to the upper end of the meadow. When the snow is stable, head up the creek between moraines. Ski up the middle of the valley to the last tree opposite the highest point of the right moraine, then turn left and traverse the relatively gentle slope to the top of the moraine. Follow the crest 100 feet, then ski through trees to a small gully which, when followed to the top of 4500 feet, gives views over the entire area.

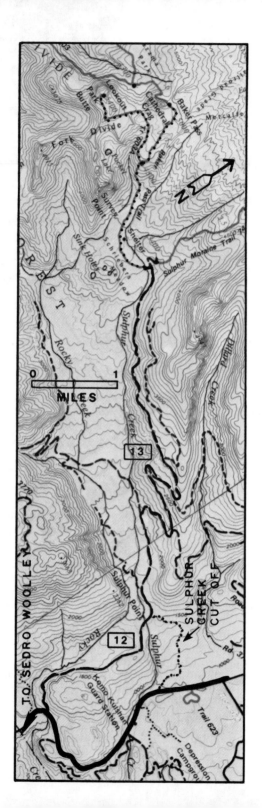

When snow is unstable, especially after a heavy accumulation, the steep moraine walls present an avalanche hazard. In this case turn left at the upper end of Schreibers Meadow and ascend the steep, narrow summer trail through forest to Park Butte.

Skier-snowmobiler "incidents" on the approach route to the meadow have stimulated the Forest Service to build a new skier trail. At this writing one section is complete, the Sulphur Creek Cutoff Trail. It starts from the Baker Lake Road 300 feet south of the Shadow of Sentinels Nature Trail Sno-Park (see Tour 13), climbs a steep and narrow road 2 miles to meet Road 12 at its 2⅓-mile mark, and follows the road to Schreibers Meadow. There will *still* be racketeers in the meadows, sad to say.

Park Butte

12 ANDERSON BUTTE

*Skill level: advanced basic on road,
  mountaineer to lakes or butte
Round trip: 10 miles to road-end
Skiing time: 5 hours
Elevation gain: 2000 feet*

*High point: 4500 feet to road-end
Best: December and mid-
  March–April
Avalanche potential: low
Map: Green Trails, Lake Shannon*

Oh, what a view! Save this trip for a clear day when you can abandon
the briefcase and the pinstripes for your skis and polypro. To really savor
the views bring along a sun hat and your lawn chair. If you prefer catch-
ing your views on the run, bring the telemark skis and carve up the
nearby clearcuts. And if you have a preference for high-elevation views
bring the climbing skins to ascend Anderson Butte.

Access: Take Highway 20 east from Sedro Woolley 14.5 miles and turn
left on the Baker Lake-Grandy Lake Road. Drive to the Baker Dam turnoff
(Forest Road 1106) and turn right. Pass a campground at 1.3 miles, then
cross the dam. At 2.2 miles from the Baker Lake Road, turn left onto Road
1107 and follow signs to Watson Lake Trail.

As the snowline varies, there is no way to predict the starting location,
but in early or late season much of the slog up the low portion of the butte

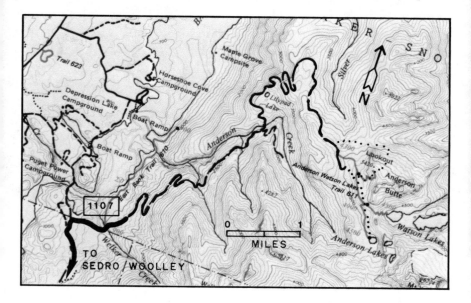

Mount Baker from the Anderson Butte Road

can be avoided. Trip mileages start from Road 1107, but with good planning and luck, you should be able to drive 4 or 5 miles beyond the turnoff, to around 2500 feet.

The Tour: From snowline, ski up Road 1107, crossing Anderson Creek 5½ miles from Road 1106 and passing Lilypad Lake near 6 miles (3000 feet). Soon after, Mount Baker comes into full view, complete with an occasional wisp of pungent steam from Sherman Crater.

The road heads into a series of switchbacks culminating at 8¼ miles (3850 feet) when Mount Shuksan, looking like a centerfold photograph, commands your attention. It doesn't get any better than this, so if you've got the lawn chair in tow, plunk it down, open a brew, and enjoy.

If lounging isn't your style, continue on. The road winds over a gentle ridge at 8½ miles where you'll obtain your first views of Anderson Butte and the glaciated mass of Bacon Peak beyond. Just ahead is a huge, north-facing clearcut which frequently holds good powder, long after the neighboring slopes have turned into slurpies. Pick a slope with a view of Mount Baker or Mount Shuksan to practice the fine art of simultaneous view watching and telemarking.

The road ends in the trees at 4500 feet, 9½ miles from Road 1106. Skiers with an altimeter, map, and compass may want to push up the valley 1½ miles to Lower Anderson Lake (4480 feet) or go right when the valley divides at the southern end of the butte and ski over a low forested saddle to Watson Lakes.

For views and a bit of challenging downhill skiing, head up to the old Anderson Butte lookout site, located on the northwest ridge, west of the actual summit. Ski up the valley ¼ mile from the end of the road, then put on the climbing skins and head uphill. With luck and a good map you will encounter the trail. If not, continue climbing, staying to the west of the steep slopes leading to the butte's actual summit. With unstable snow conditions, do not venture beyond the edge of the trees.

The summit of Anderson Butte is too steep and corniced for interesting skiing, so from the old lookout site (5420 feet) head down the north side of the butte, descending to about 4200 feet. Once low enough to cross below a sharp ridge to the west of the descent slope, go left. Ski west over a low pass, then contour southwest for ¾ mile back to the road.

13 MARTIN LAKE–MOROVITZ LOOP

Skill level: advanced basic
Round trip: 11–30 miles
Skiing time: 1–4 days
Elevation gain: 1600 feet
High point: 2600 feet on Boulde
  Ridge

Best: January–mid-April
Avalanche potential: none
Maps: Green Trails, Lake Shannon
  and Mount Shuksan

A 4-mile approach leads to an 11-mile loop through quiet forest with sidetrip options to views, a waterfall, and a hot springs.

Access: Drive Highway 20 east from Sedro Woolley 14.5 miles and turn left on Baker Lake-Grandy Lake Road. Drive past Koma Kulshan Guard Station to the Sno-Park at the end of the plowed road at Shadow of Sentinels Nature Trail (1000 feet). (In April or in low-snow years drive 4 miles more to parking at the Boulder Creek bridge.)

The Tour: Ski the highway through deep forest for 4 miles. Just after crossing the Boulder Creek bridge (1040 feet) go left, on Martin Lake road No. 1130, which climbs gently with occasional windows to Baker Lake

Baker Hot Springs

and Mount Shuksan. At 1½ miles (1275 feet), the road splits. To the left is Boulder Creek Road, the first of several "must" sidetrips, a climb of 1300 feet in 4 miles to clearcuts with views of Mount Shuksan, of Park Glacier flowing from the summit of Mount Baker, and over Baker Lake to Anderson Butte and Hagan Mountain.

The right fork, Road 1130, descends ½ mile to cross Park Creek, then climbs 2½ miles to meet Morovitz road No. 1144 (at 1600 feet). Here is the second sidetrip, to Rainbow Falls: Go left ½ mile uphill, then right on a forest trail ½ mile to the falls.

The loop goes right on Road 1144, for a downhill mile to the next attraction, Baker Hot Springs. Due to sanitation problems, the Forest Service removed all facilities, but the trail and hot sulfur pool remain. From the parking area negotiate a short flight of steps on the right side of the road and ski the nearly level trail ¼ mile to the springs.

The loop continues 3 more miles down Road 1144 to reach the main road at 13 miles from the Nature Trail parking lot. Ski right 2 miles to close the loop at the base of Road 1130, then 4 miles back up the highway to finish the trip at 19 miles or—if all the sidetrips are taken—30 miles.

View over the Baker Lake Valley from Boulder Creek Road

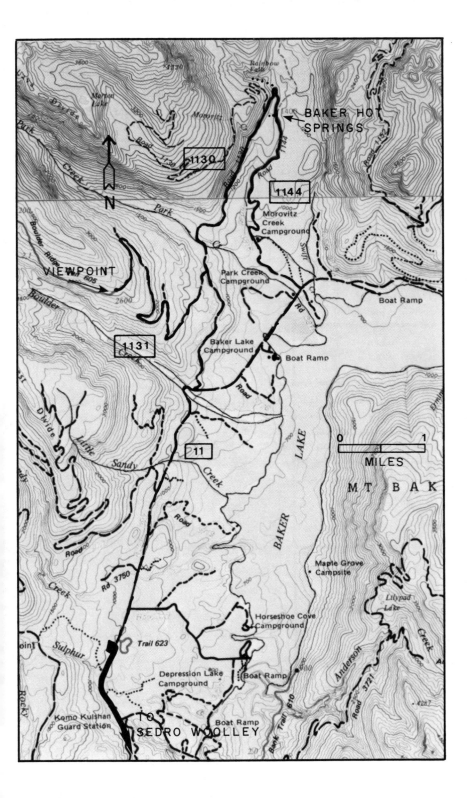

14 MOUNT SHUKSAN

Skill level: mountaineer
Round trip: 11 miles
Skiing time: 8 hours
Elevation gain: 6000 feet
High point: 8400 feet

Best: March–May
Avalanche potential: moderate
Maps: Green Trails, Mount
Shuksan; USGS, Mount
Shuksan

Telemarkers take note: the south-facing Sulphide Glacier on Mount Shuksan offers experienced skiers a 6000-foot run over moderate to steep slopes! As if that weren't enough, the Sulphide Glacier is an extraordinarily scenic tour on a spring day, when blue skies accentuate the full-on view of Mount Baker, Mount Blum, Bacon Peak, Sauk Mountain, Glacier Peak, and the other dignitaries of the North Cascades.

Although the skiing is relatively easy, the numerous natural hazards—like avalanche slopes and crevasses—pose a real threat to the inexperienced. Wands to mark the route in case of bad weather, avalanche beacons, and shovels for every member of the party are necessary pieces of equipment on this mountain.

Access: Drive Highway 20 east from Sedro Woolley 14.5 miles and turn left on the Baker Lake–Grandy Lake Road. Drive to the Koma Kulshan Guard Station, then continue on Forest Road 11 for 9.7 miles. Go left on Road 1152 and head uphill for .2 mile before taking the first fork on the right. Drive 3 miles up a series of switchbacks. Turn right on Road

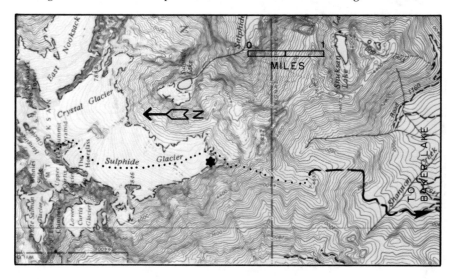

The descent

(1152)014 and go about a mile to where the road is blocked by brush or snow. Park here (2400 feet).

The Tour: Ski or hike along the old road crossing Shannon Creek then head around the shoulder of the hill, to reach the base of a clearcut at 1 mile. Ski up the open slopes to the ridge top at 4600 feet. Head north along the ridge following snow-covered Shannon Ridge Trail through heavy timber for a short mile to open meadows and campsites.

When the ridge you have followed runs into a steep, west-facing slope, turn right (east) and head up the slope to a col on the ridge above. This steep hillside is prone to sliding after heavy snowfall, strong wind, or during a warm afternoon in the sun.

Reach the col and traverse northeast for 500 feet across the steep and avalanche-prone slope between two bands of cliffs. **Note:** This is the most hazardous section of the tour. Do not ski here after a snowfall or in the heat of late afternoon. If in doubt, turn back at the col.

Past the cliff, the slope broadens; turn north and ski up to the terminus of the Sulphide Glacier. The gradient of the slope rapidly decreases as you climb, and campsites are numerous on the left (west) side of the slope. Head north, slopes will become a bit steeper above 6600 feet and level off again around 7200 feet. This entire section follows the glacier, so watch for crevasses throughout.

The summit pyramid is very steep and rocky and skied only by the crazed willing to crash and burn big-time or out-ski the avalanche they generate. Life-loving skiers can contour east around the base of the summit pyramid to the ridge beyond. Turn around at about 8400 feet.

On the way down follow your ascent route as closely as possible to avoid unseen crevasses and unsuspected cliffs. Remember to head down early to avoid possible slides caused by the afternoon heat.

15 FINNEY CREEK

Skill level: advanced basic
Round trip: 5–14 miles
Skiing time: 2–8 hours
Elevation gain: 500–2200 feet
High point: 4400 feet

Best: January–March
Avalanche potential: moderate to
low
Maps: Green Trails, Darrington and
Oso

Finney Creek is an area you must visit in the winter and only in the winter. In the summer Finney Creek Valley looks like the perfect backdrop for a movie about life on earth after an atomic war. However, when the clearcuts and stumps are covered with a soft cloak of white, the valley is a magical winter wonderland. There are miles of roads to ski, clearcuts just waiting to be telemarked, and sweeping views of the North Cascades.

A mainline logging road has opened up the entire Finney Creek Valley for exploration. There are six spur roads climbing out of the valley that make excellent winter tours. The first spur starts at a very low elevation and the last quite high, allowing skiers to follow the snowline up the valley from midwinter right into springtime.

Access: Drive Highway 20 to the sign marking the western city limits of Concrete (don't be confused by a store–service station complex on the outskirts). Turn right on the Concrete–Sauk Valley Road and follow it across the Skagit River and upstream. At 10 miles from Highway 20 turn right on Finney Creek road No. 17, a one-lane paved road with turnouts.

The First Spur: When the snow level is low, drive or ski up Finney Creek 3 miles to where Road 17 is crossed by a private logging road (790 feet). Ski the left fork, and after 4 miles of climbing on the private road reach the 3000-foot level and great views over the Skagit Valley.

The Second Spur: At 5.5 miles the second spur goes right on private land (770 feet). This road climbs 2 miles to 1800 feet and to a good view of Mount Baker.

The Third Spur: At 8 miles find Road 1705 on the right (1200 feet). This spur switchbacks 7 miles to the 3800-foot crest of Leonards Ridge and a spectacular view of Baker, Shuksan, and mountains up and down the Skagit. Bring a Forest Service map to identify them all.

The Fourth Spur: At 10.5 miles (1600 feet) is Gee Point road No. 1720, which winds more than 10 miles into the mountains, climbing to 4200 feet on the side of Gee Point, then into the Pressentin Watershed.

The Fifth Spur: At 11.5 miles the main road crosses Finney Creek. At

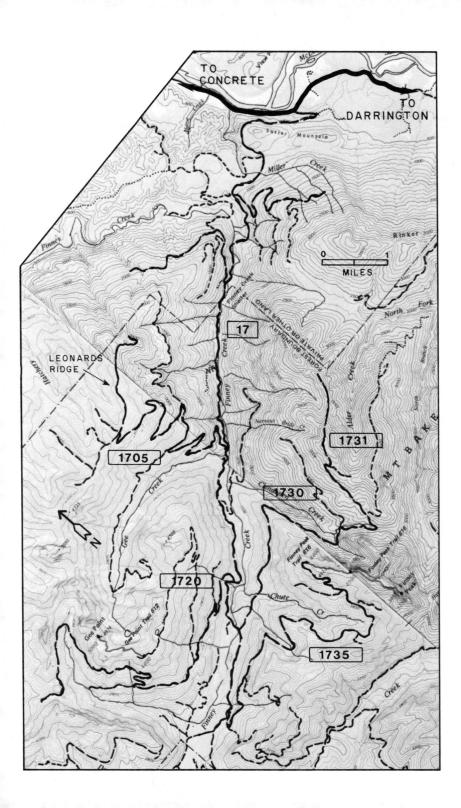

Skiing in the clearcut slopes above Finney Creek

11.8 miles it reaches Road 1730 (1800 feet), the most scenic of the six spurs. The road climbs steadily, traverses under the impressive face of Finney Peak, and at 7 miles crests a 4400-foot knoll where the views encompass all the North Cascades from Whitehorse Mountain to the Twin Sisters. If planning to ski to the knoll, be sure to have a map to identify the endless peaks. This road crosses several avalanche chutes and should not be attempted during periods of avalanche hazard.

The Sixth Spur: At 13 miles (1900 feet), the road splits. The lower road crosses into the Deer Creek drainage. Ski the left fork (Road 1735), which climbs 7 miles to a basin (4200 feet) on the west side of Finney Peak.

16 SAUK MOUNTAIN

Skill level: intermediate
Round trip: up to 12 miles
Skiing time: 6 hours
Elevation gain: up to 3200 feet
High point: 4000 feet and up

Best: January–February
Avalanche potential: high beyond
*   mile 6*
Maps: Green Trails, Lake Shannon
*   and Darrington*

"Beautiful but potentially dangerous" is an apt description of the ski tour up the Sauk Mountain Road. After skiing it once, you'll want to do it again, soon. Best be careful of developing a fatal attraction—avoid the Sauk Mountain area during and after any heavy snowfall. Also avoid the upper bowl, beyond the 7-mile mark, when the Forest Service reports indicate the slightest avalanche hazard or when sunshine warms the hillside above.

Access: Drive Highway 20 east toward Rockport State Park. At .1 mile west of the park turn north onto the Sauk Mountain Road and drive to the snowline. The tour description starts from Highway 20 (475 feet), although skiing generally starts up higher.

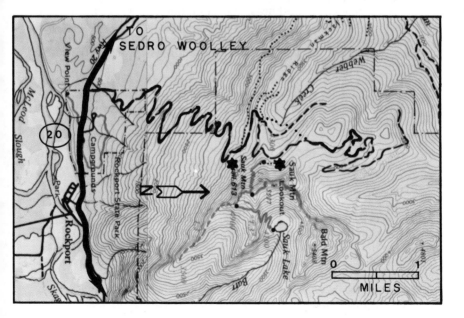

Avalanches frequently sweep across the upper portion of the Sauk Mountain Road.

The Tour: If you are lucky enough to start skiing at Highway 20, the climb is gentle as the road heads due north through heavy timber. Near the end of the first mile, the road enters a large open clearcut and starts climbing steeply. Near 1½ miles the road forks, at the corner of a switchback. Take the left fork, completing the switchback. Continue a zigzag ascent to the top of the clearing.

After 3 miles the road reenters the forest, but continues climbing steadily. The good views begin 6 miles above Highway 20, as you escape momentarily from the trees to look south over the Sauk River Valley toward Suiattle Mountain and Glacier Peak then west over the Skagit River Valley to the Puget Lowlands.

The road now makes a swing east, skirting the base of Sauk Mountain—above are the vertical avalanche chutes, descending the 2000 feet from the summit in a single long drop. If the avalanche potential is medium or high, turn around here (3400 feet).

The road traverses the base of Sauk Mountain, then swings away in a final long switchback, returning to the mountain at mile 7, where a major intersection marks an ideal turnaround point (3900 feet). From the intersection the left-hand fork traverses above the Webber Creek drainage for 1 mile to a view of Mount Baker. The Sauk Mountain Road continues climbing on up to 4000 feet, then swings across an open and *extremely* hazardous basin. Unless you know that the snow is stable and that no sun will strike the upper basin, do not continue past this point.

17 OAKES CREEK

Skill level: intermediate
Round trip: up to 16 miles
Skiing time: 5–8 hours
Elevation gain: up to 3700 feet

High point: 4100 feet
Best: January–mid-March
Avalanche potential: low
Map: Green Trails, Marblemount

A low-elevation start makes Oakes Creek the kind of tour that varies with each visit. When the snow level is low the tour begins in the moss-hung rain forest at the valley floor. When the snow level climbs, your trip starts in the open clearcuts with excellent views of the northern Cascades.

Tours starting down at the valley bottom require more skiing skills than those starting farther up. For the first 3 miles the road climbs nearly 2000 feet. Anyone who is not sure of their stopping techniques should wait until March for this tour.

Access: From Marblemount, drive Highway 20 east 4.9 miles, then turn left on Bacon Creek road No. 1060. Go up Bacon Creek Valley 1.4 miles and turn right on Oakes Creek road No. 1062. The tour description starts from this intersection (400 feet).

As there is no logging taking place on Oakes Creek Road at this time (1988), the road has been put into mothballs by the Forest Service and is cut by numerous water bars. Low-slung cars must park at the intersec-

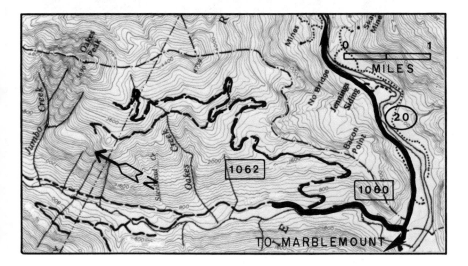

Diobsud Buttes from Oakes Creek Road

tion; however, most vehicles can clear the water bars and drive to the snow.

The Tour: From the intersection the road climbs steeply up the forested hillside. The first mile is the steepest. At the end of the second mile, the road turns north for a long traverse. Shortly after passing the third milepost (2200 feet) you will enter a huge clearcut.

The views begin as soon as you reach the clearcuts. At first all you can see are the Diobsud Buttes on the opposite side of Bacon Creek. As you climb your view extends north up the valley to the glaciers of Bacon Peak.

At 5 miles the road divides. Stay to the right on Road 1062 and continue the climb. The road ends at 8 miles (4100 feet) beneath Oakes Peak with views south to Lookout Mountain and Little Devil Peak.

18 CUTTHROAT CREEK

Skill level: advanced
Round trip: 11 miles
Skiing time: 7 hours
Elevation gain: 2300 feet
High point: 6800 feet

Best: November and late May–June
Avalanche potential: moderate
Map: Green Trails, Washington
  Pass

The first and last ski run of the season can be taken on the sheltered slopes below Cutthroat Peak. Most of the winter the North Cascades Highway is closed and the area can be reached only after an 11-mile slog up the road. No loss. By midwinter this beautiful area transforms itself into a buzzing playground with snowmobiles flitting around like insects and avalanches raining down the hillsides like heaven's avenging fly swatter.

So time your visit just before the North Cascades Highway closes for the winter or right after it reopens in the spring.

Access: Drive the North Cascades Highway (State Route 20) either 4.7 miles east from Washington Pass or 10.8 miles west from Early Winters. Turn off the main highway at Cutthroat Creek road No. 400, and drive 1 mile to the Cutthroat Trailhead (4500 feet).

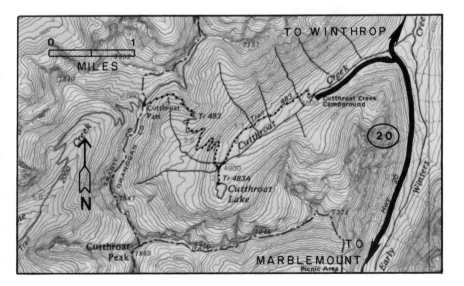

Porcupine Creek Basin

The Tour: The lower portion of the trail may be snow-free, so be prepared to carry the skis for the first mile. The trail leaves the parking lot from the horse ramp, heads up valley for several hundred feet, then crosses Cutthroat Creek on a substantial bridge. On the north side of the creek the trail makes a gentle switchback, then heads directly up valley. In a wooded area at 1¾ miles the trail forks (4900 feet). The left-hand fork continues on ¼ mile to Cutthroat Lake. The right-hand fork, Trail 483, heads up toward Cutthroat Pass and the ski slopes. If you should lose track of the trail under the snow, continue climbing straight up.

About 1½ miles from the Cutthroat Lake junction the trail enters the meadows and it is time to start planning the day's fun. Avoiding the rocky ridge tops, switchback northwest to the rounded ridge crest at 6800-foot Cutthroat Pass.

Bowls on either side of the pass provide excellent skiing. On the west side of the pass, ski across the Pacific Crest Trail and down through the upper reaches of Porcupine Creek Basin.

19 KLIPCHUCK– NORTH CASCADES HIGHWAY

Skill level: basic
Round trip: 6 miles
Skiing time: 3 hours
Elevation gain: 700 feet
High point: 2900 feet

Best: mid-December–February
Avalanche potential: low
Maps: Green Trails, Mazama and
Washington Peak

The North Cascades Highway (State Route 20) is the most romantic road in the state. The road climbs past Ross Lake then over two high mountain passes before descending along steep cliffs to the old western town of Winthrop. Extreme avalanche danger near Washington Pass necessitates closing the North Cascades Highway to automobiles during the winter, but this does not prevent winter use of the road by skiers and snowmobilers. There is no safe way around the areas of extreme avalanche danger, however, and in the winter it is the user's responsibility to stay away from the hazardous areas. This tour to Klipchuck Campground does not venture into any of the known avalanche areas. If considering traveling beyond the bounds of this trip, contact the North Cascades National Park office.

For those of us on a budget the road offers a chance to ski without having to own a Sno-Park ticket (in 1988) or paying a trail-use fee. In addition, there is very little elevation gain, making the tour ideal for first-time skiers and skaters. Unfortunately, snowmobilers find the road as appeal-

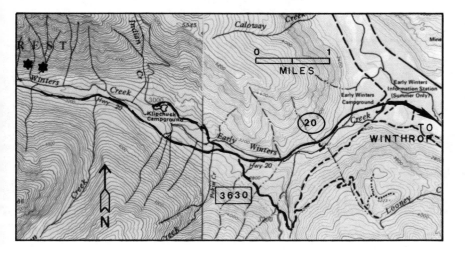

Early Winters Creek

ing as skiers do; so don't expect the air waves to be as pristine as the scenery.

Access: Drive the North Cascades Highway west from Winthrop, past Early Winters, to the end of the plowed road (2200 feet).

The Tour: Usually the best trail for skiers is along the shoulder of the highway, away from the speeding snowmobiles. However, at times it is necessary to venture onto the rutted, groomed snowmobile track.

At about 1½ miles cross Early Winters Creek and at 2 miles reach Cedar Creek Road, the first of the two side roads. Skiers with little time to spare can branch left on Cedar Creek road No. 3630 and climb the forested slopes away from the majority of the snowmobiles. You'll gain 500 feet over the next 1½ miles and end your trip at the washed-out bridge over Cedar Creek.

Skiers en route to the campground should continue on up Highway 20 ¼ mile, turn right, and ski another mile to Klipchuck Campground. You'll find lots of open campsites here if you're in the mood for some winter camping, and plenty of unoccupied tables for picnicking.

METHOW RIVER

20 CASTLE RANCH LOOP

Skill level: basic
Round trip: 5½ miles
Skiing time: 3 hours
Elevation gain: none

High point: 2240 feet
Best: January–mid-March
Avalanche potential: none
Map: Green Trails, Mazama

Old farm buildings, open fields, dry snow, and a marked ski trail. If it weren't for towering cliffs of the Goat Wall, the scene might be somewhere along the backroads of New England. Instead, it is the Castle Ranch Loop of the Methow Valley. The trail is on private land that the owners have opened to skiers but closed to snowmobiles. Please be respectful visitors; admire the quaint old buildings, but don't explore them. If you meet the owner, be sure to thank him for his hospitality.

Castle Ranch Loop is part of a network of trails maintained by the Methow Valley Ski Touring Association. Skiers must purchase a trail pass, good for any trail on the Methow Valley, to ski here. Passes may be obtained at ski shops in Twisp and Winthrop or at local resorts.

Access: Drive Highway 20 west of Winthrop 17 miles to the end of plowing at Early Winters Campground (2240 feet). Park beside the highway. A plowed county road runs north through the campground area to farms farther up the valley. The loop starts 100 feet west of this road.

Prepared tracks are perfect for kick and glide.

Castle Ranch Loop

The Tour: For a scant ¼ mile the loop trail parallels the road in the trees, then crosses to the east side. Follow blue diamonds and ski tracks through narrow strips of forest and across fields. After ¾ mile of peaceful skiing, the trail splits. The right fork leads to the North Cascades Base Camp, reached by skiing across the sometimes frozen Methow River.

For the loop take the left fork and glide for quiet miles past farms and fences; the occasional sound of rockfall on the Goat Wall is the only reminder that this is *not* New England but the Northwest. At its north end the loop meets the county road at Castle Ranch. Continue ½ mile up the valley, circling a large fenced field at 3 miles. The return leg goes along the west edge of the valley back to the starting point at Early Winters Campground.

21 RENDEZVOUS PASS VIA FAWN CREEK

Skill level: intermediate
Round trip: 13 miles
Skiing time: 6 hours
Elevation gain: 1665 feet

High point: 3985 feet
Best: December–February
Avalanche potential: moderate
Map: Green Trails, Mazama

It's like a little piece of Norway with open mountain views, well-groomed routes, and several huts, all in a *skiers only* area. Since the area is maintained by the Methow Valley Ski Touring Association, a fee is charged for the use of the area—which reminds you you're still in the States. For overnight use of the huts, contact Methow Valley Central Reservations (see Tour 25 for details).

Access: Drive west on Highway 20 from Winthrop 8.5 miles. Turn right just before crossing the Methow River and continue toward Mazama for 1.8 miles. In an area of new homes, turn left on Forest Road (5215)100, which climbs steeply past several houses. At 1 mile, after avoiding a few right turns, find the Sno-Park area (2320 feet) on a high vantage point

Skier near the Fawn Creek Hut

overlooking the Methow Valley. The access road is steep and often slippery and if your car cannot manage it, do not block the road or a private driveway.

The Tour: Skiing up the steep grade of Road (5215)100 requires considerable determination for the first 1½ miles, during which time 1140 vertical feet are gained. At your rest stops study the open slopes along side the road for the perfect telemark descent. At 3460 feet, the road branches. Just below the left fork a trail heads around a shoulder of the hill to the Fawn Creek Hut and a delightful view of Gardner Mountain to the west and Rendezvous Mountain to the south. Keep to the right and continue straight ahead into the Fawn Creek drainage on a level road.

After 2 miles, the road begins a shallow dip to the West Fork Fawn Creek, followed by a long, easy descent into Rendezvous Basin and an intersection with the Cassel Creek Road at 3100 feet. Continue on Road (5215)100, climbing through the gentle basin between Rendezvous Mountain and Grizzly Mountain. At 4¾ miles meet Road 5215 (3529 feet). Turn left and start climbing toward the pass.

Rendezvous Pass (3985 feet) is buried in trees but, by following the signs to the hut (⅛ mile northwest), you'll snag views of Gardner Mountain and the surrounding countryside.

Advanced skiers with proven ability to assess the avalanche hazards will note the possibility of a shortcut for the return, avoiding the long descent through Rendezvous Basin. From Rendezvous Hut, traverse northwest on Road (5215)150 until it starts to climb up to the ridge tops. Continue to traverse at about 4000 feet, skiing through a narrow gully between a 4251-foot knoll and the steep slopes of Rendezvous Mountain.

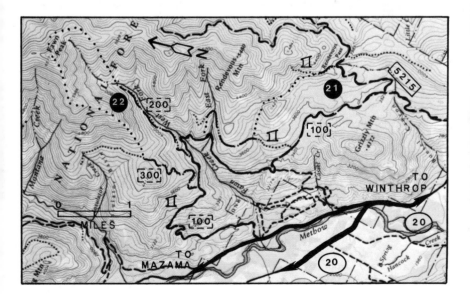

Past the knoll meet Road (5215)130 and continue traversing to a second knoll. Aim southwest and ski down a moderately steep, exposed rib. Cross Road (5215)125 and continue down to the groomed tracks on Fawn Creek road No. (5215)100. Remember, this is not a safe route unless the snow pack is stable.

22 FAWN PEAK

Skill level: mountaineer
Round trip: 12 miles
Skiing time: 8 hours
Elevation gain: 4257 feet
High point: 6577 feet

Best: mid-December–March
Avalanche potential: low
Map: Green Trails, Mazama

See map on page 71.

Ask a group of skiers which peak offers the best view in Washington and there will be a heated debate and no consensus. We expect the jury to be out for a long time on this one because the competition is incredibly tough. However, even if Fawn Peak does not have the best view in Washington, the panorama from the summit is a 360-degree masterpiece.

Three approaches offer access to the peak: the southwest rib, the West Fork Fawn Creek Basin, and the high route from Rendezvous Pass. The first two approaches can be skied in a long day and are discussed below. The approach from Rendezvous Pass is at least a two-day affair and is discussed in Tour 25.

Access: Drive Highway 20 west from Winthrop 8.5 miles. Just before crossing the Methow River go right toward Mazama for 1.8 miles. Watch for signs on the right-hand side pointing toward skier parking and head up steep Forest Road (5215)100 for 1 mile (bypassing a turnoff on the right at .5 mile) to the parking area at 2320 feet. The road to the parking area is steep so if you cannot make it, do not block the road or a driveway.

The parking lot and trail are maintained by the Methow Valley Ski Touring Association (MVSTA)—so be sure to have your pass handy.

The Tour: Ski up the double tracks of groomed West Fawn Creek road No. (5215)100. The road is steep and climbing skins may be handy from the start. After 1½ miles at the first major junction (3460 feet), a trail branches left to the Fawn Creek Hut, Just above the trail is Road (5215)300. This is the turnoff for the Ridge Route.

If skiing the Ridge Route follow Road (5215)300 as it climbs to a 4180-foot saddle. Here, leave the road and head roughly north along the ridge crest. The first chance to mark progress is a 5986-foot rounded knoll about ¾ mile from the summit. Make a short descent and then a final push to the top (6577 feet).

View of the Methow River Valley and North Cascades from Fawn Peak

The alternate approach via West Fork Fawn Creek Basin continues along Road (5215)100 for another ½ mile from the Ridge Route junction and takes the next road left (No. (5215)200). The road parallels the West Fork while climbing steeply. At 4600 feet, enter a tree plantation in an open basin. Cross the first of two small creeks here, and immediately start climbing through the planted rows of trees to the open slopes. The destination is now the ridge above (5780 feet). Once on the ridge ski left, northwest, to the summit of Fawn Peak.

Oh! What a view. It simply does not end. Even a small party will rapidly track the area as one skier after another crisscrosses and circles the summit. The peaks of the Pasayten, rounded in summer, are massive under their coats of snow. The high North Cascades are dominated by Gardner, Silver Star, Tower Mountain, and Azurite Peak. Finally the Methow Valley and Okanogan Mountains unfold at your feet.

For the descent, the basin route frequently offers the best snow as it holds the powder long after it has blown off the Ridge Route.

23 LEWIS BUTTE

Skill level: intermediate
Round trip: 3½ miles
Skiing time: 2 hours
Elevation gain: 1050 feet
High point: 3346 feet
Best: January–February
Avalanche potential: low
Map: Green Trails, Doe Mountain

Summit of Lewis Butte

   This tour starts in a delightful country setting among farms, fields, and old barns. Proceed up open slopes while planning where you will weave multiple sets of telemark tracks on the way back down. Once at the top of Lewis Butte it is easy to forget about the ambitious itinerary you planned in favor of a long lunch followed by some discreet sunbathing (discreet because you will probably have company).

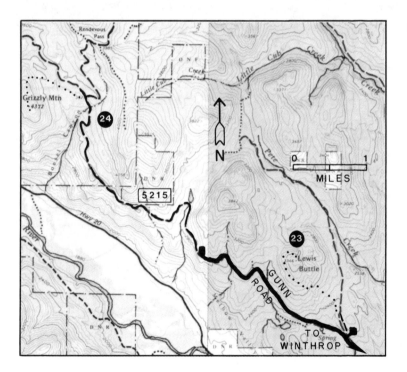

Unfortunately, the wide-open spaces that make this such an excellent skiing area also attract snowmobiles. While the racket may be distracting, there is plenty of room to steer clear of the machines and find your own slopes to molest. If annoyed by the snowmobiles, try skiing here midweek. Maybe you'll be blessed with silence.

Access: From Winthrop go west on Highway 20, and in .2 mile go right on West Chewack River Road. After another mile turn left on Rendezvous Road, and drive 1 mile to the Gunn Road junction and an unofficial snowmobile parking area. Park here (2300 feet)—there are no other wide places.

The Tour: Lewis Butte, the largest hill in the immediate vicinity, rises like a large scoop of vanilla ice cream northwest of the junction. Pick your own route up the butte, avoiding snowmobile tracks, climbing with a series of zigzags at whatever steepness is comfortable. At approximately 1½ miles reach what appears to be the top, but isn't. The true summit is another ¼ mile farther. Drop a bit and then climb another 200 feet to the 3346-foot summit of Lewis Butte.

A word about the Methow Valley. The snow almost always comes down as powder. A day or two of warm weather or rain transforms the snow cover into a firm base. However, some years the temperatures never get above 20°F all winter and on shady exposures the snow never consolidates, so skiers can find themselves waist deep in wonderful powder scraping rocks and sagebrush. This is rarely a problem on south-facing slopes which receive the winter sun, but be careful on those north-facing slopes.

Methow River Valley

24 METHOW VALLEY VIEW

Skill level: basic
Round trip: 5 miles
Skiing time: 3 hours
Elevation gain: 700 feet in, 200 feet out
High point: 3300 feet

Best: January–February
Avalanche potential: low
Map: Green Trails, Mazama

See map on page 74.

Bird's-eye views of the Methow Valley and a great backdoor entrance to the popular Skier Only trails of the Grizzly Mountain–Rendezvous Pass area highlight this tour. The rolling hills of the eastern Cascades offer beginners an excellent playground. Keep in mind, however, that icy conditions can transform the undulating terrain into a hairy roller-coaster ride.

Access: Drive west from Winthrop for .2 mile on Highway 20, then turn right on West Chewack River Road for 1 mile. At Rendezvous Road, also called County Road No. 1223, go left and drive 1 mile to a fork. Go left on Gunn Road for 3.4 miles to a turnaround where the plowing ends. Usually you'll find a turnout just big enough to park one or two cars (2800 feet).

The Tour: Beyond the parking spot the county road makes a horseshoe bend as it circles a farm field, rounds a bend in the hillside, goes up a short, steep pitch, and enters the forest. At 1 mile reach the brink of a steep cliff with an aerial view of the Methow River 1000 feet below. The valley is only half the view; across the way Gardner Mountain gleams under a coat of snow and ice.

From the viewpoint the route enters the woods. Half a mile farther, the road enters the National Forest and the county road becomes Forest Road 5215. At 2½ miles you'll intersect the groomed Fawn Creek–Rendezvous Pass ski trails near Grizzly Mountain. To ski the 1¾ miles to Rendezvous Pass on Road 5215 you need a Methow Valley Ski Touring Association pass. If you are an advanced skier and wish to continue on, without a pass, ski the untracked slopes of Grizzly Mountain. The most popular approach heads north around the base of the mountain and ascends the north ridge to the 4372-foot summit. After fresh snowfall the descent is a classic.

Farms below Lewis Butte

25 RENDEZVOUS PASS HUT TO HUT

Skill level: advanced basic
Round trip: 10 miles
Skiing time: 1–4 days
Elevation gain: 1345 feet
High point: 3985 feet

Best: mid-December–February
Avalanche potential: none
Maps: Green Trails, Doe Mountain
  and Mazama

   Anyone who has ever spent several long winter nights in a tent will immediately recognize the appeal of hut-to-hut skiing. The Rendezvous Outfitters offer a system of four huts connected by groomed ski trails in the hills north of Winthrop. It's like a little piece of Norway tucked away in our own backyard.

Rendezvous Hut

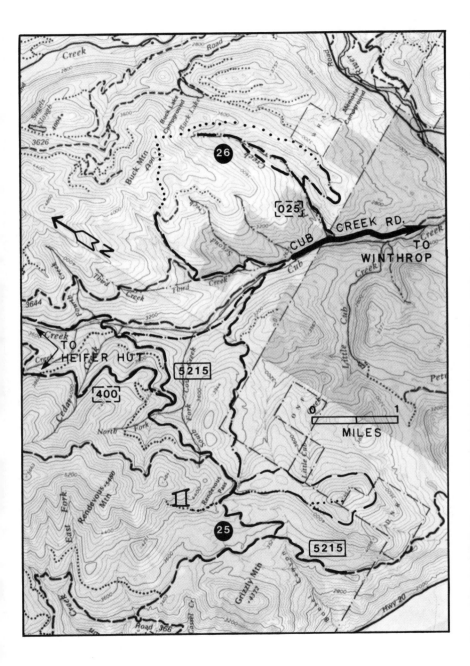

Besides the huts, which take the sting out of winter camping, the Rendezvous Pass area offers excellent touring on groomed trails, backcountry exploring, and outstanding slopes for telemarking.

The Rendezvous Pass area is part of the Methow Valley Ski Touring Association Trail System and a pass must be purchased before skiing on the trails. Reservations and information can be obtained by calling Methow Valley Central Reservations at 1-800-422-3048. Pack and gear hauling services are also available if you're into ultralight skiing.

Tours to Rendezvous Pass start near Mazama at Fawn Creek or from the east at Cub Creek. For the Fawn Creek access see Tour 21. The Cub Creek access is the shortest to Rendezvous Pass and the best for day trips.

Access: Drive Highway 20 west .1 mile from Winthrop. Turn right on West Chewack River Road and drive 6.6 miles to Cub Creek Road. Turn left and drive 2.5 miles to the parking area at the end of the plowed road (2840 feet).

The Tour: Ski up Cub Creek Road (now called Forest Road 52). After ½ mile, the road divides. The right fork leads to Buck Mountain (see Tour 26). Follow the left fork ⅛ mile down to Cub Creek; then take the first road on the left and cross the creek. Ski up this road 300 feet to another fork and go right on spur road 370 (the left fork is the Little Cub Creek Trail, one of two possible return routes).

The route heads up the valley on a nearly level trail through forest and meadow for 2 miles until it meets Road 5215. Turn left here and ski uphill into the South Fork Cow Creek Valley.

Zipping down a groomed ski trail from Rendezvous Pass

Four miles from the start spur road (5215)400 branches off on the right, part of the Cedar Creek Loop which leads to Banker Pass and the Heifer Hut (an alternative return route). Continue straight up Road 5215. Pass the upper end of the Little Cub Creek Trail at 5 miles. After another 200 feet, the Cougar Mountain Loop Trail takes off on the left—this trail is an alternate loop approach to Rendezvous Hut but is 3 miles longer.

Rendezvous Pass is reached at 5½ miles (3985 feet). The pass area is in trees. For views east and west ski to the left a few hundred feet up a small knoll. To reach Rendezvous Hut, ski over the pass about 300 feet then follow the trail markers to the right (off the road) into the forest for ½ mile.

For those staying at the hut, miles of marked trails lead out from the pass area, such as the 5-mile groomed track around Cougar Mountain, a 13-mile round trip to Fawn Peak, or a long descent to the Methow River Valley past the Cassal Hut and Fawn Hut (see Tour 21).

The return may be made by Little Cub Creek or Cedar Creek. The trip back by Little Cub Creek is 4½ miles long on a steep trail that is difficult to ski when icy. Cedar Creek Loop is a 10-mile ski from the pass back to the parking area. The trail is not steep and the views of Buck Mountain make this an excellent tour for long-distance skiers.

METHOW RIVER

26 BUCK MOUNTAIN LOOP

Skill level: advanced
Round trip: 10 miles
Skiing time: 7 hours
Elevation gain: 1900 feet
High point: 4490 feet

Best: mid-December–March
Avalanche potential: low
Map: Green Trails, Doe Mountain

See map on page 79.

Buck Mountain is a perfect example of all things that have made the Methow Valley famous among cross-country skiers—open slopes for telemarking, peaceful countryside for touring, and vistas of the North Cascades and the Pasayten Mountains.

Skied from either the southwest or southeast, the two legs of the route join for a loop separated by a .1-mile road walk. The southwest leg crosses open slopes and may be telemarked almost nonstop from the top to the valley floor. The southeast leg offers two different ways, both scenic, to complete the loop. The following description is for skiers who want a scenic trip up and a long fun-filled run down.

Access: Drive Highway 20 north .1 mile from Winthrop. Turn right on West Chewack River Road for 6.6 miles, then turn left on Cub Creek Road

Open slopes near the summit of Buck Mountain

for 2.5 miles to the end of plowing (2840 feet). Walk back down the road .1 mile and turn left (north) on Forest Road (5200)025 just past First Creek.

The Tour: After crossing a cattle guard, the road climbs steeply up a narrow valley. At ¾ mile (2900 feet), the road splits. To the right a scenic ridge route, longer by 2 miles, leads to the top. To the left is a shorter, but still beautiful, valley route.

Valley Route: The left fork splits again in ¼ mile. Take either left or right; they rejoin in 1 mile, forming a small loop. At the head of the valley the road ends, leaving a short, steep climb up the side of an open slope to the north to join the ridge route.

Ridge Route: The right fork climbs gently, rounding the ridge, to the road-end at 2 miles (3200 feet). Follow blue diamonds on a traverse up to the ridge top, bypassing the first summit. Continue north, keeping a little right (east) of the ridge crest. At 3700 feet the route climbs the west side of a major knoll, then heads to Buck Mountain summit at 5 miles (4490 feet).

The views extend far and wide. The Chewack River Valley, Paul Mountain, and Cougar Mountain are only a few of the sights. On a clear day the impressive peaks of Gardner, Midnight, and Oval are visible.

The downward route chosen will depend on the skier's ability. Begin by descending southwest, following the blue diamonds to meet a forest Service road at 3680 feet. Ski on down, staying left at all intersections, to close the loop in 3 miles. To challenge your telemarking skills, ski this road ¼ mile from the top until a stock-loading ramp and corral are visible far below. Head down to this corral, dropping 1160 feet in almost nonstop skiing. From the bottom, follow the road down and back to your car.

27 BUCK LAKE

Skill level: intermediate
Round trip: 6 miles
Skiing time: 3 hours
Elevation gain: 1080 feet

High point: 3200 feet
Best: December–February
Avalanche potential: low
Map: Green Trails, Doe Mountain

Buck Lake lies on a wide bench below Buck Mountain, west of Doe Mountain, east of Fawn Peak, north of Blue Buck Mountain, and not far northwest of yet another Buck Mountain. At least it is a change from all those early explorers who named the summits after sweethearts, friends, politicians, or themselves.

Despite the overworked name, Buck Lake makes a delightful destination for a short day tour. The lake with its fish, boat ramp, and campground are buried under a still, white blanket of snow.

Fence near Buck Lake Campground

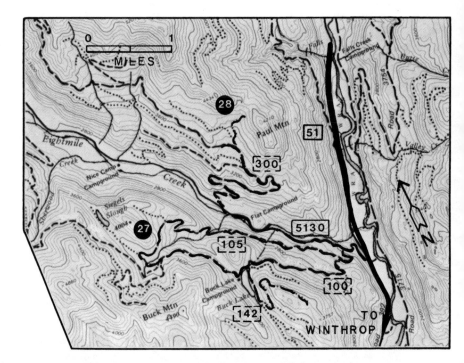

Access: Drive to Winthrop on Highway 20. When the highway makes a 90-degree turn in the center of town, leave the main road and continue straight north on County Road 9137. After 6.8 miles cross the Chewack River, and join the West Chewack River Road, which becomes Forest Road 51. Continue upriver another 2.5 miles to Eightmile Sno-Park located just opposite Eightmile River road No. 5130.

The Tour: Eightmile River Road is a groomed snowmobile route. Luckily, throughout the week and on most weekends few machines use it and skiing is quite pleasant. The road starts at 2120 feet and begins to climb immediately, making a couple of switchbacks before reaching the Buck Lake turnoff on the left, in a short mile (2360 feet).

The Buck Lake road No. (5130)100 continues to climb steeply, promising a fast descent for the return trip. At 1½ miles pass a semiabandoned logging road on the right and continue to climb. Around 2 miles the road straightens and traverses northwest through logging cuts. Across the valley you'll see Paul Mountain with its rocky walls and very little snow.

At mile 3, the road divides again. The left fork leads to the south end of Buck Lake, the boat ramp, and eventually to the summit of a low hill overlooking the lake on spur road (5130)142. The right fork heads to the campground.

If more exercise is desired, 4 extra miles may be added to the tour by skiing rarely used logging roads in a long loop. Starting from Buck Lake, ski to the right, past the campground, for 1½ miles. The first time the road divides stay right on Road (5130)100. The next times it divides, go right on Road (5130)105. Stay on this road as it loops east, then bends south, returning to the Buck Lake Road 1½ miles from the Sno-Park. Few views or snowmobiles bless or curse this loop.

METHOW RIVER

28 FLAT CAMPGROUND AND PAUL MOUNTAIN

Skill level: advanced basic
Round trip: 4 miles to Flat
  Campground
Skiing time: 2 hours
Elevation gain: 440 feet

High point: 2560 feet
Best: January–mid-March
Avalanche potential: moderate
Map: Green Trails, Doe Mountain

See map on page 84.

It's a case of Dr. Jekyll and Mr. Hyde. High in its valley, Eightmile Creek flows calmly, almost lazily, below snowcapped mountains. Snowbridges span the creek along its meandering course. Suddenly, the character of the creek changes, as it approaches the rocky valley wall above the Chewack River. The creek unleashes its fury as it gushes, bubbles, and carves its way down to the Chewack.

This tour follows schizophrenic Eightmile Creek from the Chewack River, up along the turbulent gorge, and into the quiet valley above with its red-barked ponderosa forests and peaceful snow-covered meadows. Skiing this area is a must for the complete Methow Valley experience and well worth the risk to life and limb. Yes, you must ski a groomed snowmobile road to get there.

Access: Drive to Winthrop on Highway 20, then continue through town on County Road No. 9137. At 6.8 miles cross the Chewack River bridge and continue up the west side for another 2.5 miles to the Eightmile Creek Sno-Park, located opposite Eightmile River road No. 5130, (2120 feet).

The Tour: Eightmile River Road climbs steadily through timber for the first mile, passing the Buck Lake Junction then leveling off to hug the precipitous walls above Eightmile Creek. Near 2 miles the road makes a shallow dip, crosses Eightmile Creek, and then climbs gently along the creek. Stay on the left (creek) side of the road here. The dirt bank on the right lets loose slides of surprisingly large porportions on wet or warm days.

Shortly beyond the bridge is Flat Campground, well named to be sure. This makes an excellent turnaround point for a short tour. Those wishing

Paul Mountain

to carry on should leave the valley floor, with its groomed road and snow-mobile traffic, and start climbing.

Ski up the valley to the second road on the right (about 500 feet beyond the campground). Head uphill on Road (5130)300, which leads to Lamb Butte and eventually to Eightmile Ridge. The best views occur after 2 miles. From the flank of Paul Mountain you'll look down on Eightmile Creek and across to Buck Mountain.

29 DOE MOUNTAIN

The Road

Skill level: intermediate
Round trip: 12 miles
Skiing time: 6 hours
Elevation gain: 2750 feet
High point: 5000 feet
Best: December–March
Avalanche potential: moderate
Map: Green Trails, Doe Mountain

The Mountain

Skill level: advanced
Round trip: 6 miles from road-end
Skiing time: 5 hours
Elevation gain: 2154 feet
High point: 7154 feet
Best: February–March
Avalanche potential: low
Map: Green Trails, Doe Mountain

Doe Mountain sports a challenging backcountry tour in late fall and spring, while its access road provides an excellent wintertime outing. This is an area with beautiful, open slopes and thin forests ignored by both snowmobilers and skiers.

Access: Drive to Winthrop, leave Highway 20, and continue north through town. City streets and tourists give way to County Road 9137, the East Chewack River Road. Cross the Chewack River 6.8 miles north of Highway 20, join the West Chewack River Road and continue north. At an unspecified point the county road becomes Forest Road 51. Doe Mountain Road branches off to the left 7 miles north of the Chewack River

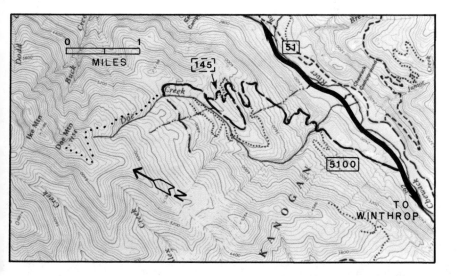

bridge. Park on the road's edge as far out of the way as possible. In 1988, no signs marked the start of Doe Mountain Road, but worry not, this is the only road heading up on the left for several miles.

The Road: Doe Mountain road No. (5100)100 starts at 2250 feet and climbs gently along a broad bench. After 2¼ miles, Road (5100)125 branches left. If looking for an early turnaround point, this is a good one. Shortly after, the road rounds a corner and heads into a deep gully to cross Doe Creek. At 4 miles Road (5100)145 branches to the right. This is a shortcut to the end of the road, overgrown in spots, with numerous unmarked intersections—definitely the direction for explorers. The main road makes a broad bend and follows Doe Creek up to a broad saddle (5000 feet). In 1987 the road was being expanded; watch for updates in future editions.

For the descent, parallel the east side of Road 5100 to Road (5100)145, cross it, and ski down its south side for an excellent run through trees and meadows.

The Mountain: To ski up Doe Mountain, follow the left fork of the road where it divides at the 5000-foot saddle. Ski this fork to a crossing of Doe Creek. The old trail is on the left side of the creek and vaguely discernible by the blazes on the trees. Follow the trail (or just parallel the creek) up to 6500 feet and swing left across the top of Doe Creek to a ridge on the far side. Now ski the ridge to the north up to an old lookout site on the summit of Doe Mountain (7154 feet).

When the sky is clear, the views from the summit are extensive. The mass of Garland Peak dominates the western vista; the Methow River Valley unfolds to the south; the rolling Pasayten summits lie to the north; and to the east you'll see North Twentymile Peak (with its lookout still intact), South Twentymile Peak, and First Butte.

View from the summit of Doe Mountain

30 BLUE BUCK MOUNTAIN

Skill level: advanced basic
Round trip: 4 miles to Cougar Lake,
* 10 miles to road-end*
Skiing time: 2–4 hours
Elevation gain: 1200 feet to lake,
* 3400 feet to road-end*

High point: 5400 feet
Best: mid-December–mid-March
Avalanche potential: low
Map: Green Trails, Twisp

Here is some good news: the forest road this tour follows cuts through the Methow Valley Wildlife Recreation Area and is closed to motors from October 1 to December 31 while the deer are migrating from the high mountains to their wintering grounds along the Columbia River. Guess when you should ski here.

Besides the possibility of seeing deer, you'll ski to views which sweep across Pearrygin Lake, the farms of the Methow Valley and up to the High Cascades.

Access: From the center of Winthrop follow the main street north on the East Chewack River Road. At 1.6 miles go right on the Pearrygin Road. At

Methow River Valley and the North Cascades

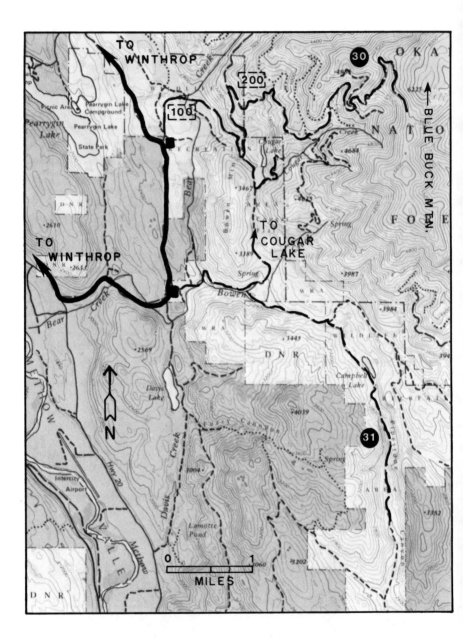

3.3 miles keep left, passing the state park entrance. At 5.3 miles find Road (5008)100 signed "Bear Creek" on the left, a gate, and a large Methow Wildlife Recreation Area sign. Park near the gate, but don't block the farmers' road on the right (2000 feet).

The Tour: Ski the road 1½ miles to the Cougar Lake Junction at the first switchback. To reach the lake go right for a short ¼ mile, then climb left to a campground and left again to the small lake (3200 feet).

Back on the main road, the route climbs gently another ½ mile to another junction. Go right on Road (5008)200 to the National Forest Boundary (3400 feet).

From here numerous side roads diverge, but provided the signs are not buried, there should be little trouble following the main road. In another mile there is a four-way junction—go straight through on Road (5008)225. At 5 miles from the plowed road (5400 feet), the road ends. Trees make it impractical for all but advanced skiers to continue to the top of Blue Buck Mountain, but the views during the entire tour make the trip very worthwhile.

Blue Buck Road

31 PIPESTONE CANYON

Skill level: intermediate
Round trip: 10 miles to head of
  Pipestone Canyon
Skiing time: 5 hours
Elevation gain: 750 feet

High point: 2900 feet
Best: January–February
Avalanche potential: low
Map: Green Trail, Twisp

See map on page 90.

Not far above the town of Winthrop an exotically beautiful canyon lies hidden amongst the open, rolling hills. Its steep walls have been carved

Skier crossing a cattle fence

by wind and water into the intriguing rock formations that give the canyon its name. Located in the heart of a wildlife preserve, Pipestone Canyon can be traveled only by those with four legs or two skis.

Access: Coming into the south end of Winthrop on Highway 20, cross the Methow River and take the first right on Main Street. In .2 mile go left on Center Street and then, in a few yards, right on Park Avenue. Drive south 1.5 miles and turn left on Bear Creek Road. Head uphill past the golf course to the pavement end in 1.8 miles. Park in a small plowed area on the right side of the road (2150 feet).

The Tour: Ski Campbell Lake Road up a narrow gully, climbing steadily. Cattle fences are crossed—it is essential that you restring them after passing through. At 2 miles, just after the second and last fence, the road forks. The left leads north around Bowen Mountain to Cougar Lake. Take the right fork east toward Campbell Lake. At 3½ miles the road enters a broad meadow (2900 feet) and continues over the ridge 4 miles to Beaver Creek road. Stay on the right side of the meadow to find the windswept road to Campbell Lake. The way descends to the south shore, the entrance to Pipestone Canyon. Continue on the road, descending the canyon ½ mile to the pipestone formation. If time allows, ski the entire 2-mile length of the canyon, losing only 480 feet. Rounded hills at the lower end offer good skiing. The quiet visitor may see deer or coyotes.

METHOW RIVER

32 SUN MOUNTAIN

Skill level: basic
Nearly 20 miles of trails
Skiing time: 3 hours–all day
Elevation gain: 1387 feet
High point: 3987 feet

Best: January–mid-March
Avalanche potential: low
Map: Green Trails, Buttermilk Butte

Sun Mountain Lodge is perched 1000 feet above the Methow Valley in the center of a network of groomed and/or marked cross-country trails that lead to scenic overlooks, mountain passes, and lakes. Whether novice or veteran, any skier will appreciate the way miles skim by on prepared tracks.

Access: Drive Highway 20 north from Twisp 5.3 miles. Turn left on Twin Lake Road for 1.8 miles, then go left on Patterson Lake Road for 5.6 more miles to Sun Mountain Lodge. Stop by the ski shop for a map, further information about trails, and a ski pass, required for all trail users. Parking at the lodge itself is for guests, but .5 mile below the lodge is a public parking area (2700 feet).

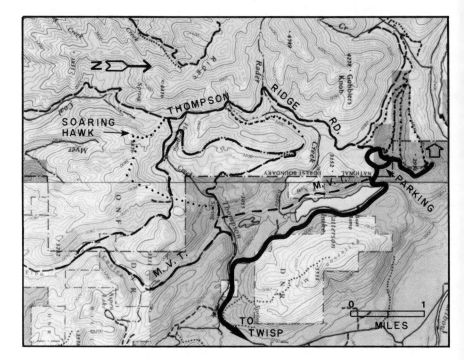

The Tour: Enjoyable day trips can be made from the lodge or public parking lot. Follow the Ridge Route to Hough Homestead Shelter or the Beaver Pond Trail to the beaver pond; telemarkers like to climb to the top of Herringbone Hill to swish down.

Soaring Hawk Loop is a combination of groomed trails and an exciting off-track route for intermediate skiers. From the public parking lot cross the main road to snow-covered Thompson Ridge Road. Stay with the groomed road 4 miles to a major intersection (3480 feet), with Diving Hawk Ski Trail. Leave the groomed trail and climb the ridge between the two roads. Pass to the left of the first knob and go across a shallow saddle. Make the final ascent to the top of Soaring Hawk at 5 miles (3987 feet).

From this high perch the view extends to hundreds of Cascade peaks, over Elbow Coulee, and across the Methow Valley. Return the way you came or do a loop, testing telemarking skills by descending the open, forested slopes of Soaring Hawk's northeast side. Ski across Diving Hawk Trail to meet Upper Pine Forest Trail; close the loop by following this trail to Cut-Off Trail, which leads to Thompson Ridge Road and back to Sun Mountain Lodge or the parking lot.

Skiers on the Beaver Pond Trail

33 METHOW VALLEY TRAIL (M.V.T.)

Skill level: advanced basic
One way: 19 miles
Skiing time: 5 hours–2 days
Elevation gain: up to 1000 feet

High point: 2600 feet
Best: January–mid-March
Avalanche potential: low
Map: Green Trails, Twisp

The Methow Valley Trail isn't what the name suggests. It's not really a valley trail at all, except that it gives grand views the length and width of the valley as it climbs to ridge tops, winds around frozen lakes, and passes overlooks. The trail is maintained and groomed by the Methow Valley Ski Touring Association (MVSTA) and a pass is required to ski here. Passes may be purchased at ski shops in Twisp or Winthrop or at local resorts.

The trail may be skied as a whole or in sections. Here the trail is described in three parts, from south to north.

Methow Valley Trail near Twisp

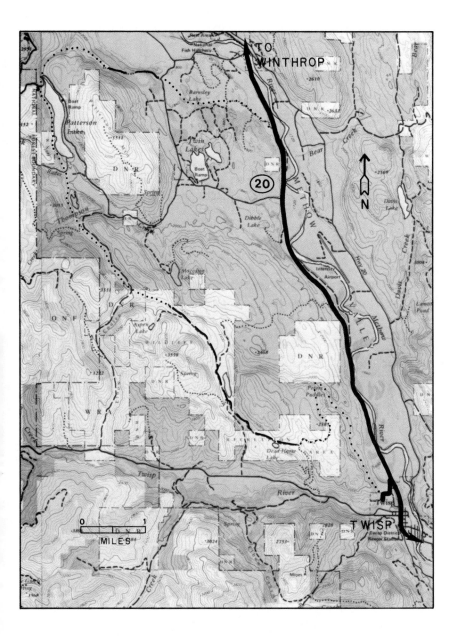

Twisp to Elbow Coulee: This 8-mile section is the most scenic traversing wild, open country with broad vistas and miles of hills to explore. A 1000-foot ascent and a steep 200-foot descent at the end make it best suited for skiers of intermediate level and up. The trail is marked by blue-painted stakes which often are difficult to spot; be sure to carry a contour map.

Drive Highway 20 north from the center of Twisp, cross the Twisp River at the edge of town, and take the first left. Follow this street .3 mile and take the first left for .2 mile. The road makes a sharp bend (1610 feet); find a parking place well off the street.

Climb north to an open terrace on an old jeep road, cross the terrace, and follow a narrow gully left. Pass to the left of snow-covered Peters Puddles and turn left up another long, open hill. At the top follow a spur road west down to Dead Horse Lake (2300 feet) at 4 miles and on to join a forest road, the route for the next 3 miles. If time allows, at the 6½-mile point make a ½-mile sidetrip to Aspen lake. At 7 miles the road ends. The final mile drops to Elbow Coulee Road (2400 feet).

Elbow Coulee to Patterson Lake: This is the least demanding section, 4 miles long, gaining only 100 feet, following a groomed trail through open timber and around Patterson Lake. Easiest access is from the north end at Patterson Lake Resort, 1 mile below Sun Mountain Lodge (see Tour 32).

Patterson Lake to Winthrop (Virginian Motel): This 6-mile section, all in open country, descends 740 feet to the valley floor. It is best for intermediate level skiers.

Park at Patterson Lake Resort and walk .1 mile along the road to the end of the lake (2500 feet). Pass through a small gate and ski down a narrow steep gully, following the markers. The trail drops 500 feet in the first mile, then turns right around the base of Patterson Mountain. Cross Twin Lakes Road at 3 miles. The final stretch, nearly level, is out in the open with views of glistening white hills to the east. The trail ends at Highway 20 (1740 feet), 1¼ miles south of Winthrop and ⅓ mile south of the Virginian Motel.

The Methow Valley Trail, designed and maintained by local citizens and businesses, crosses both public and private land; please respect property rights.

34 LOUP-LOUP

Skill level: basic　　　　　　　　　*High point: 4100 feet*
Round trip: 4 miles or more　　　　*Best: December–February*
Skiing time: 3 hours　　　　　　　　*Avalanche potential: none*
Elevation gain: 100 feet　　　　　　*Map: Green Trails, Loup-Loup*

What better place to ski a loop than on the Loup-Loup? Actually the name may have nothing to do with circles, but rather stems from the French word for wolf (*loup*); whether or not this particular *loup* ran in circles through the open forest is a fact that has been lost in history.

Loup-Loup Trail, maintained by the Methow Valley Ski Touring Association and the Ide-A-Wile Inn, is regularly groomed and is signed with blue diamonds. Though terrain is rolling, the way maintains a near-constant elevation. Numerous sidetrips to ridge tops or along roads can extend the tour to a long day or several long days.

Access: Drive Highway 20 to Loup-Loup Pass (4000 feet), located 10.5 miles east of the junction of Highways 20 and 153 and 18 miles west of Okanogan. Park at the summit in the plowed space on the south side of the highway.

The Tour: Ski the South Summit Road, a combination skier-snowmobile route. In a scant ¼ mile an overlook gives views down the

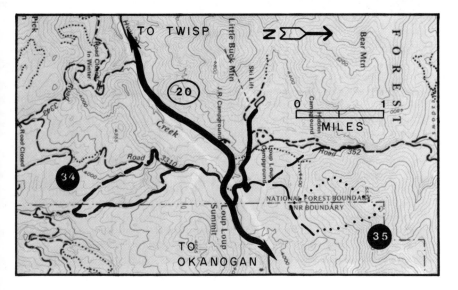

Methow Valley from Loup-Loup Trail

length of Fraser Creek to magnificent peaks of the North Cascades. In another long ½ mile is an intersection where snow machines are directed to the right; skiers turn left and climb a short, steep hill to the start of the loop. To avoid chaos with the other skiers, do the loop in a clockwise direction.

At the top of the hill bear left. (The trail to the right will be the return leg.) Cruise through open timber where animal tracks abound; watch for rabbit tracks followed by coyote tracks. Unless directed otherwise, at junctions with all the numerous side roads stay right for the basic loop. (Supplied with an up-to-date Forest Service or Green Trails map, skiers can explore these untracked side roads on great loops lasting several days.) The Loup-Loup trail meanders through quiet forest with many attractive spots for a picnic. The loop closes at 3¼ miles and the final ¾ mile follows the road back to the summit parking area.

35 TELEMARK MOUNTAIN

Skill level: advanced
Round trip: 6 miles
Skiing time: 4 hours
Elevation gain: 1512 feet
High point: 5532 feet

Best: January–March
Avalanche potential: moderate
Map: Green Trails, Loup-Loup

See map on page 99.

A steep climb without an established trail leads to far views. Telemark Mountain has good snow the whole season but is especially noted for fine spring skiing. The steep slopes have an 800-foot vertical drop, perfect for sweeping runs. Energetic skiers may repeat the trip several times in an afternoon.

Access: Drive Highway 20 east from Winthrop toward Okanogan. At .3 mile past Loup-Loup Summit turn north on the access to the downhill ski area, .1 mile to a Sno-Park (4020 feet).

Telemark Mountain

Coyote tracks in the snow

The Tour: Before starting out take some time to get a feel for the terrain because beyond the road-end the navigation through the trees is strictly seat-of-the-pants. To the north the large hill with open slopes and a few trees crowning the summit is Telemark Mountain. The route follows the west ridge to the top.

Head north from the Sno-Park, as do most of the machine tracks. The machines themselves are rarely on hand except on weekends, when they arrive in large packs. However, Methow Valley snowmobilers are some of the most polite in the country; stay to the side of the road and your space will be respected.

Keep count of not-so-obvious spur roads to the right. Take the third; if you come to a major forest road, you've gone too far—turn around and recount. Follow this spur about 1 mile, then ascend to the ridge and ski northeast along the crest. Just before the main mass of the mountain, dip off the crest briefly to round a small rock haystack. The summit (5532 feet) provides an overlook of a good portion of the Okanogan country, miles and miles over rolling hills almost to the Columbia River.

In good weather and stable snow, descend open slopes on the south to a small basin, then contour west (right) to rejoin your uphill tracks. During times of high avalanche hazard go down the way you came up—no hardship because it also is good skiing.

36 BUCK MOUNTAIN LOOKOUT

Skill level: intermediate
Round trip: 9 miles
Skiing time: 5 hours
Elevation gain: 2675 feet

High point: 6135 feet
Best: January–March
Avalanche potential: moderate
Map: Green Trails, Loup-Loup

Telemarkers note: Skiing the southern slopes below Buck Mountain Lookout after winter storms dump a load of powder will put a grin on your face. The spring skiing here, after the sun has thawed the corn, is equally delightful. The telemarking is so much fun you may care less about the views which, incidentally, are excellent.

Access: Drive Highway 153 up the Methow River Valley to Highway 20 and turn east 3 miles before Twisp. Drive to the summit of Loup-Loup Pass and then proceed down the east side 2.7 miles to a road on the north side of the highway signed "Buck Mountain Road." Limited parking here allows space for four cars if everyone packs together or a maximum of two small cars if not. (Do not take any more space than necessary; some folks like to release their parking frustrations by taking a key and S-C-R-A-T-C-H-I-N-G it along the length of the offending vehicle.)

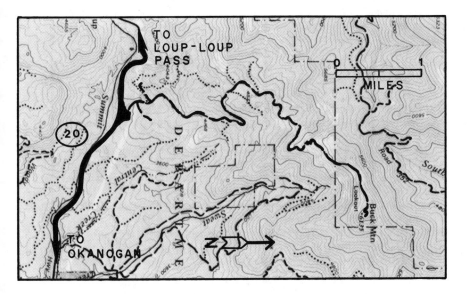

Buck Mountain Lookout

The Tour: Buck Mountain Road begins climbing at 3460 feet and in its first mile passes several well-signed intersections, first with Powerline Road followed by Summit Creek Road. Later intersections are not so well signed. To add to the confusion, Buck Mountain Lookout Road is on state land, where the road numbering is a bit haphazard. The road starts as B100, changes to OM B1000, and eventually has no number at all. Carry a good topographical map, and consult it when in doubt.

After 1½ miles of steady climbing the road eases off on a broad bench. After Central Creek Road joins on the left (4120 feet), Buck Mountain Lookout Road switchbacks up to a narrow saddle, then levels off again, contouring northeast for a mile into an open basin.

At 3 miles you'll reach an unmarked intersection (4900 feet). Stay right and climb to an open ridge crossing atop the first of several good telemarking slopes. The route is now obvious because the lookout is visible. The road is frequently covered by snowdrifts, so simply stay to the east side of the ridge until directly below the lookout. Here the narrow road leads straight up to the summit with its 360-degree views.

Buck Mountain Road

37 SMITH CANYON

The Road

Skill level: basic
Round trip: 3 miles
Skiing time: 2 hours
Elevation gain: 400 feet
High point: 3100 feet
Best: mid-December–February
Avalanche potential: low
Map: Green Trails, Twisp

The Ridge

Skill level: advanced
Round trip: 5 miles
Skiing time: 3 hours
Elevation gain: 1800 feet
High point: 4200 feet
Best: mid-December–February
Avalanche potential: moderate
Map: Green Trails, Twisp

No pass or permit is required to enjoy this tour along a quiet Forest Service road tucked away from the mainstream of winter recreation in the Methow Valley. Novices will enjoy this short, gentle road while the bowls at road's end will keep advanced-level skiers busy for hours while sketching snake-like signatures down the open slopes.

To date, few skiers have discovered this area, and snowmobiles are rare—probably because the road is too short and the hills too steep.

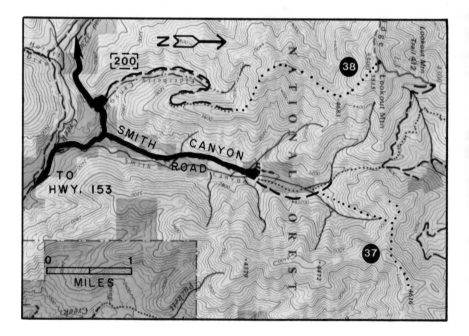

Smith Canyon Road

Access: Drive east on State Route 153 for 1.2 miles from the town of Carlton. Turn right on a county road signed "Libby Creek." At 2.4 miles keep right on Chicamun Canyon Road. At 3.6 miles from Highway 153, go right again on Smith Canyon Road and 5.3 miles from the highway—at the entrance to "The Little Ponderosa" ranch—park (2700 feet). Be sure your car does not block the driveway or obstruct local traffic.

The Tour: About 100 feet before the ranch gate, find a logging road on the right. Follow it as it climbs through forest to open meadow at 1 mile. Views open up all around. Gaze over the ranch at the edge of the meadow, down Smith Canyon, to the Methow Valley. Across the valley the tower on Lookout Mountain is visible. When the road reaches an obvious high point it appears feasible to leave the road and climb the open slope to the 4400-foot ridge of Lookout Mountain.

However, the route described here continues on the road, losing 200 feet in the next ½ mile. Near the lowest point where the road crosses a culvert is the end of "The Road" section of the tour. Beyond lie the open slopes and ridge top.

For open-slope skiing, go right, climbing ¼ mile to a corral. From here either follow a wide foot trail to the left along the creek bottom and then switchback up steep slopes to the ridge top or, if there is enough snow to cover the rocks and sagebrush, climb directly up the open slopes to a 4200-foot high point on the ridge.

No matter which way the ridge is reached, the views of the Cascade giants are disappointing. Trees completely cover the north side of the ridge, so after spending time looking for a window between the branches, turn around and enjoy the downhill run that makes this trip so worthwhile.

A note about the snow. For off-road skiing in this area you need a couple of feet of snow to cover the small brush and rocks. Snow accumulations of 2 to 3 feet make for excellent skiing. However, accumulations of over 3 feet are unstable on the steeper, open slopes. Years with heavy snowfall are few and far between in the Methow, but potentially very dangerous when they occur. If there has been heavy snow buildup, stay off all steeper open slopes (including the slopes of Smith Canyon), skiing only on the ridge tops. If unfamiliar with this area, check on avalanche hazards at the Twisp Ranger Station before starting out.

38 ELDERBERRY CANYON

Skill level: intermediate
Round trip: 5 miles
Skiing time: 3 hours
Elevation gain: 1400 feet
High point: 3786 feet

Best: January–February
Avalanche potential: low
Map: Green Trails, Twisp

See map on page 106.

The Elderberry Canyon Road is fairly short and generally ignored by snowmobilers. Their loss is our gain and skiers can enjoy a peaceful tour here, even on weekends.

The logging road traveled climbs quite steeply and can be hazardous when icy, so we recommend the tour for intermediate skiers. Advanced skiers will also appreciate the access to nearby telemarking slopes.

View toward Hoodoo Peak from Elderberry Canyon

Leave fences as you find them.

Access: Drive State Route 153 east of Carlton 1.2 miles and turn onto a county road signed "Libby Creek." At 2.4 miles keep right on a road signed "Chicamun Canyon" and at 3.6 miles go left. At 4 miles from the highway find the Elderberry Canyon Road, also known as Forest Road (1046)200. Usually you'll find a small, plowed turnout here for parking (2362 feet).

The Tour: The road climbs steadily for 1½ miles along the forested floor of Elderberry Canyon. At 3100 feet, the road crosses from the west to the east side of the canyon and climbs up the hillside to the ridge top. As the road climbs, the Sawtooth Range pokes over the horizon. Once on the ridge top you're rewarded with additional views of the Methow Valley, the fire lookout building on Lookout Mountain, and the snow-covered ridges above Smith Canyon. At about 2½ miles, the road ends at the foot of a rounded hill (3788 feet). Before turning around, ski a little higher on the open slopes to the left for the best views.

In good weather advanced skiers can continue on climbing to the top of the open slopes and follow the ups and downs of the ridge crest to the top of Lookout Mountain, approximately 1½ miles farther and 1700 feet higher.

39 COOPER LOOPS

Ridge Loop

Skill level: advanced
Round trip: 6 miles
Skiing time: 4 hours
Elevation gain: 2200 feet
High point: 4828 feet
Best: January–February
Avalanche potential: moderate
Map: USGS, Cooper Ridge

Road Loop

Skill level: intermediate
Round trip: 10 miles
Skiing time: 5 hours
Elevation gain: 2372 feet
High point: 5000 feet
Best: mid-December–February
Avalanche potential: low
Map: USGS, Cooper Ridge

It was really hard singling out a trip in this area because logging roads, skid roads, and jeep roads honeycomb the surrounding hills. Also, the endless open slopes seduce skiers to abandon the roads in favor of ex-

The Ridge Loop

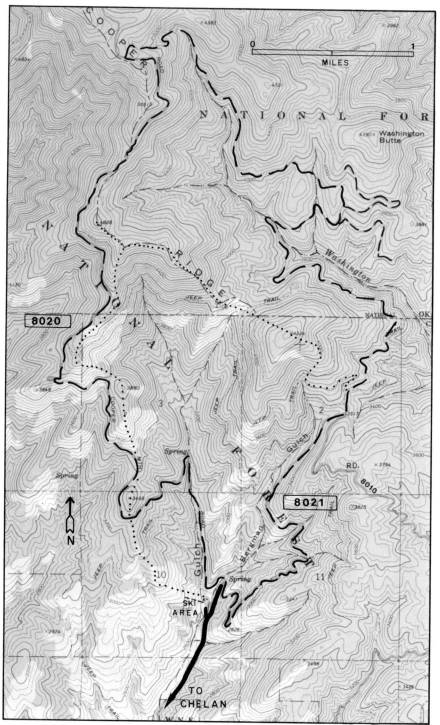

ploring the open ridges and surrounding peaklets. Try the loops mentioned below and then formulate another 20 tours of your own making.

Access: Drive 4 miles from the center of Chelan on State Route 150 along the north shore of the lake, then go right (uphill). Follow signs for 7.4 miles to the Echo Valley Ski Area, where a rope tow and poma lift keynote the facilities. There are also about 6 miles (10 kilometers) of groomed cross-country ski trails. Leave a donation before skiing on the Echo Valley Trails.

Drive past the ski area to the snowmobile Sno-Park. Park here (2628 feet).

The Tour: The Road Loop begins at the upper end of the Sno-Park. Ski uphill on Road 8021 (there is no trail fee for this area). The road climbs up Bergman Gulch 2 miles to its first major intersection with Road 8010 from Purtteman Gulch (3517 feet). Continue north, winding circuitously around several ridges and crossing Washington Creek at 4 miles (3400 feet). About ½ mile beyond the creek is the first of two important intersections. At the first, go left (3800 feet). At the second, ⅛ mile beyond, go left again, remaining on Forest Road 8021.

Climbing now becomes serious business as the road works its way steadily up the Washington Creek valley. Several spur roads are passed, but with the objective (Cooper Ridge) directly ahead the route is obvious. Cooper Ridge is crested at 5200 feet and Road 8021 meets Road 8020. Go left, heading down the ridge on Road 8020. Close the loop by gliding back down Cooper Ridge on Road 8020 with its excellent views south of Lake Chelan and Mount Stuart. The road makes its final descent along the edge of Echo Valley Ski Area, ending at the Sno-Park.

The Ridge Loop begins the same as the Road Loop. From the upper end of the Sno-Park ski up Road 8021 for 2 miles to the first major intersection. Now leave the road system and climb (west) up to the summit of a high, open ridge (4324 feet). Ski down (west) over several skid roads to the next saddle and up to the highest point beyond (4828 feet). You are now on Cooper Ridge, straddling the line between Chelan and Okanogan counties. Once you're saturated by the view, follow the ridge line as it rolls south toward the ski area, avoiding Road 8020 as much as possible. The final descent may be made on Road 8020 or down the steep ski area slopes.

40 ANTILON LAKES

Skill level: basic
Round trip: 3 miles
Skiing time: 2 hours
Elevation gain: 150 feet

High point: 2300 feet
Best: December–February
Avalanche potential: none
Map: USGS, Manson

A short trip with very little elevation gain makes for lots of fun for young or novice skiers. A campground at the far end of two small lakes provides a good destination.

Access: From Chelan's city center, turn onto Highway 150 and drive west along Lake Chelan's shoreline, heading toward the town of Manson.

Gray day at Antilon Lakes

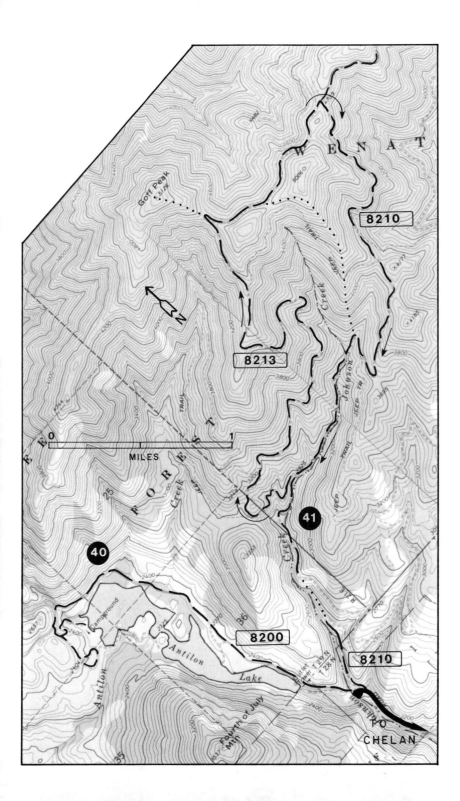

At 6.8 miles, opposite the entrance to Old Mill Park, turn right on Wapato Lake Road. Wind up through apple orchards for 2.4 miles, then turn right on Upper Joe Creek Road, which turns into Forest Road 8200 and arrives at the Sno-Park in 3.9 miles (2150 feet).

The Tour: Ski up Forest Road 8200, gaining most of the elevation in this short, quick stretch. On the left, an earth dam marks the start of the first Antilon Lake. The road contours along the east shore, turning farther east as it rounds the second lake. Above, the hillsides are steep and barren— logged, burned, or both.

As the road begins another climb, note the steep road heading down to a clump of trees and campground at the upper end of the second Antilon Lake. If this looks too steep for comfort, continue on about 500 feet to a second access with a more reasonable grade.

Many skiers and even snowmobiles go straight across the lakes and connecting stream, ignoring the road in this section. When the lakes are frozen solid with a coating of new snow, this is great sport. Practice kick-and-glide or skating across the sleek surface. However, be cautious before venturing out onto the lake. If you fall through, you probably won't get out.

Winter's delicate beauty

Summit of Goff Peak

41 GOFF PEAK

Skill level: intermediate
Round trip: 10 miles
Skiing time: 5 hours
Elevation gain: 2966 feet
High point: 5126 feet
Best: December–February

Avalanche potential: moderate
Maps: USGS, Manson and Cooper
Ridge

See map on page 115.

See map on page 115.

    Two routes lead to Goff Peak and its magnificent views. The intermediate tour follows roads the entire way and may be skied as a loop. Meanwhile, advanced skiers can weave the roads and open slopes into a tour that offers refuge from the whining snowmobiles.

Access: Drive to the Antilon Lakes Sno-Park (see Tour 40 for directions).

The Tour: For the intermediate tour, start from the Sno-Park and walk 500 feet back down Forest Road 8200 to Road 8210. Begin skiing north up the groomed snowmobile raceway paralleling Johnson Creek. Fire and logging have left the surrounding hillsides barren, so views commence immediately.

The route leaves Road 8210 at the first switchback and continues straight ahead on an abandoned jeep road, eliminating a mile of meandering on the main road. Climb rapidly along Johnson Creek and after a mile arrive at a small basin and a much better road. This is Road 8213; go left and follow it for the next 4 miles.

Road 8213 climbs steadily, becoming steeper as it nears the top. Numerous spur roads branch off; however, the main road can generally be identified by its lack of road-number signs. Near the top all road signs disappear, making the right choice a real guessing game in a snowstorm. Goff Peak is to the north and slightly west of the other hills, so near the top, veer left and up at all intersections.

The road reaches a narrow saddle at 4750 feet. Goff Peak is the small hill to the left. Ski up to the 5126-foot summit—the view is outstanding. To the northeast lies Cooper Mountain, one of many points of note on Cooper Ridge. To the west are the Chelan Mountains from Pyramid Mountain to Stormy Mountain rising high above the rest. Far below lie miles of orchards along the shores of Lake Chelan.

For the return trip, consider throwing yourself for a loop. From the 4750-foot saddle, ski south, then east, contouring a full mile to meet the groomed snowmobile route on Road 8210. The descent is obvious and fast the entire way down.

For advanced skiers with climbing skins and a yearning to explore, a fun way to approach Goff Peak is up the ridge tops and over the open slopes. To avoid the extremely steep slopes, start from the Sno-Park and ski up Road 8210. Do not branch off at the switchback; stick with it for about 2½ miles. The road follows a broad, open valley with a small creek in the center. Note where the road crosses from the south to the north side of the creek, then contour east for about ½ mile. When the road turns south, head uphill to the summit of a high, open ridge. The first summit is 4185 feet. Continue north-northwest to a small saddle and then climb up to a 5006-foot hill. Now follow the ridge line west to the logging road at the 4750-foot saddle below Goff Peak.

42 BEAR MOUNTAIN RANCH

Skill level: basic
40 kilometers (25 miles) of groomed
* trails*
Skiing time: 1–2 days
Elevation gain: up to 1400 feet

High point: 3400 feet
Best: December–February
Avalanche potential: none
Maps: USGS, Chelan and Winesap

If views are as much your passion as skiing, you're going to have trouble getting anywhere at Bear Mountain Ranch. Views intrude in every direction. The ski area overlooks Lake Chelan, a host of snow-

Lake Chelan from Bear Mountain Ranch

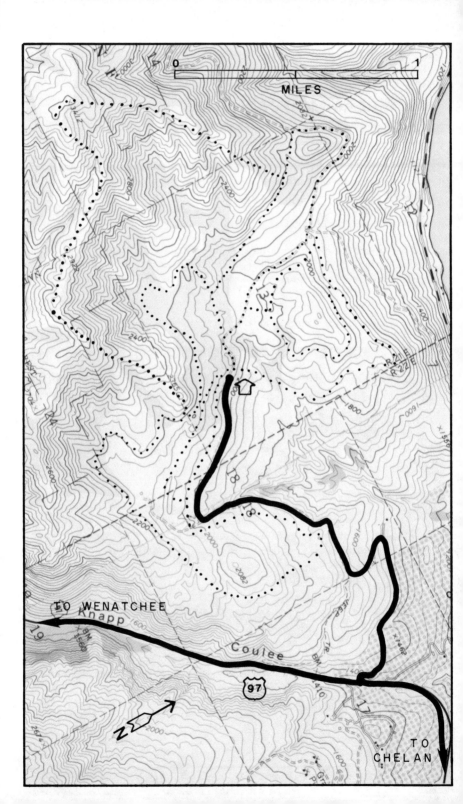

Skiers in the groomed trails at Bear Mountain Ranch

capped mountains, and miles of apple orchards. The ski trails wind from viewpoint to viewpoint while skimming through pine forests, climbing over high ridges, and cruising through meadows and ranch fields. Besides the distant views, this area also exposes you to close-up views of old homesteads and ranch lands.

Bear Mountain Ranch is a working ranch during the summer. But in the winter, the owners groom 40 kilometers (25 miles) of trails with a Piston Bully. The trails are double tracked with a skating platform in the center. The area also offers ski rentals, some refreshments, a warming "hut" (actually a yurt), and limited overnight accommodations.

The resort is open Friday through Sunday and on holidays throughout the ski season. A fee is charged to ski the resort trails, which are open from 10 A.M. to 4 P.M. Skiers must be out by 4:30, when the entrance gate is closed.

Access: Drive Highway 97 north from Wenatchee and start counting miles after the tunnel. After 4.3 miles, watch for the backwards "BMR" brand on the left side of the highway and follow the single-lane dirt county road 2 miles up to the ranch parking area.

The Tour : Try the Parking Lot Loop to warm up and then venture onto the more exotic Quail Run or Wolf Hollow before heading over to Lakeview Trail and on. Trails are rated for Beginners, Intermediates, Experts, and Telemarkers. The highest trail climbs up to the top of 3400-foot Bear Mountain, followed by a run down that is definitely for experts only.

Green Mountain

43 GREEN MOUNTAIN

Skill level: mountaineer
Round trip: 8 miles from road-end
Skiing time: 6 hours
Elevation gain: 3000 feet
High point: 6530 feet

Best: December and May
Avalanche potential: moderate
Map: Green Trails, Downey
   Mountain

Because of a long road approach and high avalanche potential through-out the winter, Green Mountain is best reserved for early- or late-season tours. As soon as the emerald meadows are covered by their first foot of snow, skiing is excellent on the steep, open slopes amid views of the North Cascades from Mount Baker all the way to a glimpse of Mount Rainier. In spring the timing is trickier. A party must wait until the road melts open and the snow pack stabilizes to solid corn, but not so long that the snow is more water than snow—or has gone into summer hibernation. The timing for views, however, is not difficult to figure. It just takes good weather.

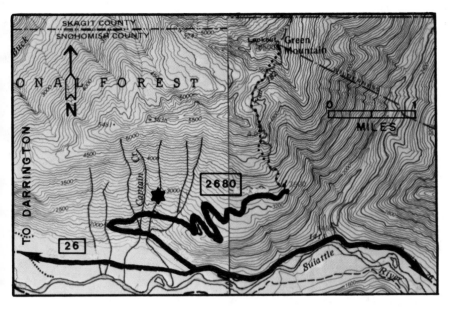

Glacier Peak from the Green Mountain ski route

Access: Drive north from Darrington or south from Rockport to Suiattle River road No. 26 and follow it 19 miles to Green Mountain road No. 2680 (1300 feet). Follow the road for 5 miles to its end (3500 feet) or until blocked by snow or slides.

The Tour: Green Mountain Trail starts on a forested hillside 300 feet before the road-end. Ski or hike the steep trail the first mile through dense timber to treeline at the edge of open meadows (4200 feet). (If the trail is lost in timber, ski steeply up from the parking lot with a slight lean to the left.)

At treeline skirt left around the edge of the meadows, keeping in the shelter of the trees and avoiding several obvious avalanche tracks. At the end of the meadows turn uphill and climb 200 feet to a slanting bench in the protection of trees.

Traverse to the right, ascending across the bench, using as much forest cover as possible. Once on the east side of the slope, ski to the ridge top. Follow the crest up another 500 feet and then traverse right to a tree-dotted shelf leading to a small snow-covered lake in a deep bowl (5220 feet).

Before reaching the lake choose your route to the lookout on the 6530-foot summit of Green Mountain. When the snow is stable, ski up the middle of the open south slope to the first saddle west of the lookout and join the ridge route for the final ascent. Unwrap the sandwiches and gaze at Mount Buckindy (just to the north). Dome Peak, Baker, and Shuksan. To the south stand Glacier Peak, White Chuck, Pugh, and Sloan.

SAUK RIVER

44 WHITE CHUCK MOUNTAIN VIEW

Skill level: advanced basic
Round trip: 10 miles to viewpoint
Skiing time: 6 hours
Elevation gain: 2150 feet

High point: 4250 feet
Best: March–April
Avalanche potential: low
Map: Green Trails, Sloan Peak

Ski to endless views of mountains, farms, and clearcuts from a 4450-foot viewpoint. If energy is boundless, continue on to the base of the towering cliffs of White Chuck Mountain. The climb is easiest on logging roads; however, on the descent you may plunge down the "man-made telemark slopes" (i.e., clearcuts).

Access: Drive north through the town of Darrington on State Route 530. Just short of the Darrington Ranger Station, go right on 288th Street NE, signed "Sauk Prairie." In .5 mile cross the Sauk River and continue on another 2.4 miles. Turn right on Forest Road 24, which climbs steeply for

White Chuck Mountain

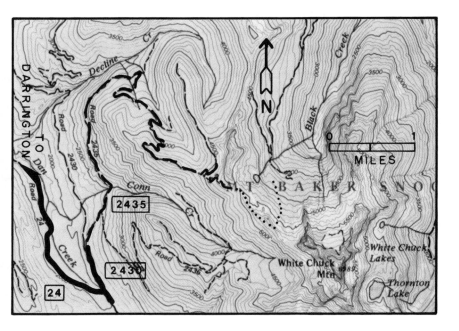

Camp Robber

3 miles, then levels off in the Dan Creek Valley. After driving 4.8 miles on Road 24 go left on Road 2430, in the middle of a big U bend. In .5 mile turn uphill on Road 2435 (2100 feet). Miles and elevation gain are calculated from this junction, but drive on to the snowline.

The Tour: Head up Road 2435 through forests and clearcuts. After ½ mile pass Road 2436 (summer climbing access to White Chuck Mountain) on the right (2700 feet). At 2½ miles pass by a spur road on the left, and begin a series of steep switchbacks. At 4½ miles reach a very narrow ridge crest which divides the Conn Creek drainage to the south from the Decline Creek drainage to the north.

The road climbs steeply to within a few feet of the 4450-foot high point and views of Mount Baker and The Sisters to the north; Higgins, Whitehorse, and Three Fingers to the west; and the Monte Cristo Peaks, Sloan, Pugh, and the towering cliffs of White Chuck Mountain (6989 feet) to the south.

The road now descends 100 feet, then swings north, contouring at a nearly constant elevation for another 2 miles to the end of a ridge overlooking Decline Creek.

Adventurous skiers should leave Road 2435 right after descending the ridge from the 4450-foot point. Continue straight as the main road swings left and follow a steep spur road up the ridgeline. The spur road ends around 4900 feet. Continue east to a saddle at 4975 feet. Turn southeast and ski the ridge for 1 mile to the top of a large open meadow at 5380 feet. Now let the skis rip and descent 500 feet through wide meadows before turning around and climbing back to the ridge.

For the descent, return to the 4450-foot point and follow the ridge crest down ½ mile or so. Then head out into the clearcuts and ski the open hills back to your car.

45 RAT TRAP PASS

Skill level: advanced basic
Round trip: 7 miles
Skiing time: 4 hours
Elevation gain: 1492 feet
High point: 3150 feet

Best: November–December and
*   March*
Avalanche potential: moderate
Map: Green Trails, Sloan Peak

Rat Trap is an inelegant name for a beautiful open pass boxed in by sheer walls which climb 4000 feet straight up to the snow-plastered summit of White Chuck Mountain. The pass is ¼ mile of open meadows surrounded by broad clearcut slopes, making it an ideal area for gazing at the views, picnicking, building snowmen, and telemarking.

The tour is entirely on a scenic logging road which cuts through the tight band of steep hills on the north side of the White Chuck River between White Chuck Mountain and Meadow Mountain. Views along the entire tour are outstanding, so pick a clear day for your trip.

Timing is crucial for this tour. It is best to plan this tour either in early winter or early spring. Midwinter skiers are faced with a long valley-bottom approach of 5½ miles or more up the White River Road from the Mountain Loop Highway.

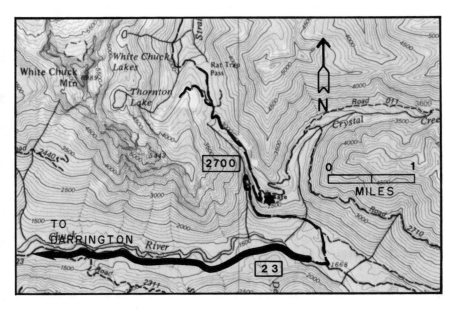

White Chuck Mountain from Rat Trap Pass

Access: From Darrington drive the Mountain Loop Highway 9 miles up the Sauk River, then turn left on the White River road No. 23. Drive up valley for 5.5 miles to Road 2700. Park here (1668 feet).

The Tour: Ski up Road 2700, climbing gradually. Two spur roads are passed in the first ¾ mile; stay left both times. At 1¼ miles there is the first of many outstanding views of Pugh and an excellent view of Glacier Peak.

Near 2 miles the road enters a narrow valley, twice crosses a boisterous little creek, then winds across a steep open hillside. Snow sloughs from the hillside above after any heavy snowfall, so use caution and common sense, and ski briskly across the exposed area.

At 2½ miles Road 2710 branches off to the east, heading to the Meadow Mountain and Crystal Lakes trailheads. A mile beyond the intersection the road makes a final switchback, then climbs into the clearcut meadows of Rat Trap Pass (3150 feet).

There are excellent views of White Chuck Mountain throughout the pass area, and at the north end there are vantage points overlooking Straight Creek drainage to the farms far below. The best views of the area are at the top of the clearcut hill on the west side of the pass. To reach this vantage point, either head straight up the hill or follow the spur road starting near the entrance to the pass. Once on top you can lay back and watch the avalanches stream down the face of White Chuck Mountain.

46 KENNEDY HOT SPRINGS

Skill level: mountaineer
Round trip: 10 miles from road-end
Skiing time: 8 hours
Elevation gain: 2300 feet
High point: 3300 feet

Best: February–March
Avalanche potential: high
Maps: Green Trails, Sloan Peak and
  Glacier Peak

Hot springs and skiing are a seductive combination, so it's not surprising Kennedy Hot Springs is a popular winter tour. A hot bath after a day of skiing soothes the back and takes the sting out of winter camping. Near the hot pool a large meadow offers a perfect tent site. Not that it matters—once you get in the water you probably won't get out.

There is no best time to ski to Kennedy Hot Springs. During a heavy snow year, a day skier may never get beyond the White Chuck River Road, because the access roads may be closed from the Mountain Loop Highway on. How much of the road is drivable varies from year to year. In a year when the snowfall is light, the trail may never receive enough snow to cover the rocks and roots, so when you leave home be sure and throw the hiking boots in, just in case.

Access: Drive to Darrington and follow the "Mountain Loop Highway" signs south. The county road turns into Forest Road No. 20 at the edge of

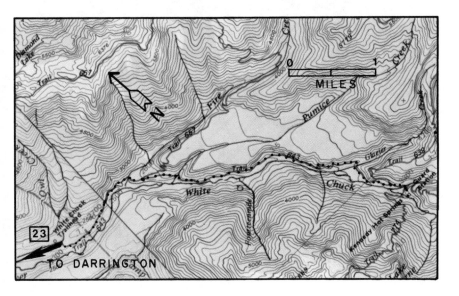

town and parallels the Sauk River. Take the second road on the left immediately after crossing the Sauk River bridge. White Chuck River road No.
23 is 11 miles long and ends at a small campground and trailhead. Park
here (2300 feet).

The Tour: The trail travels upriver, tunneling through thick brush and
around tall trees for ¾ mile, and then climbs above the river along a steep

Kennedy Hot Springs

hillside. After 1½ miles descend to Fire Creek and pass the Meadow Mountain Trail. Cross Pumice Creek at 2 miles. From here the trail descends to the river and crosses a beach area covered with boulders freshly dislodged from the hillside above. Do not linger: this is a hazardous area.

Shortly beyond, the trail crosses an open bank directly above the river. The trail slides off this slope every year and the snow does not hold well. If the bank looks questionable, retreat to a broad slope and ascend, cross over the top of the bank, and then return to the trail. A little farther on there is one more hazardous bank. This one must be crossed, frequently on foot. Keep alert for the minor slides that do occur here.

At 4 miles the trail makes a single switchback, a notable landmark, then enters an open flood plain and crosses several creeks, arriving at Kennedy Creek at 5 miles. Across the creek go right to the guard station (3300 feet). The hot-springs pool is across the White Chuck River and reached by a bridge. Proceed across with caution as there is only a handrail on the upriver side and it is frequently obscured by piles of snow.

Go left and walk 50 feet to the steaming pool, which is fairly warm throughout the winter (it does cool off during the spring snowmelt, though). Just don't stand there now, get in.

SAUK RIVER

47 NORTH MOUNTAIN

Skill level: advanced basic
Round trip: 2–28 miles
Skiing time: 2 hours–2 days
Elevation gain: up to 3000 feet
High point: 4000 feet

Best: January–April
Avalanche potential: low
Map: Green Trails, Darrington

The North Lookout Road offers views from lazy, damp valley bottoms to a crisp polar display of Whitehorse, Higgins, Pugh, Glacier Peak, White Chuck, Mount Baker, and even the Pickets. The numerous spurs provide destinations suitable for whatever amount of time is available and from wherever the snowline may be.

Access: Drive Highway 530 to Darrington. Continue on the highway north .7 mile past Darrington Ranger Station and turn left on paved Road 28. At 2.5 miles is a major intersection (1000 feet), the usual winter starting point for skiers.

The Tour: The right fork, Road 2810, heads toward Texas Pond and North Lookout, the recommended destination when the machine-sitting

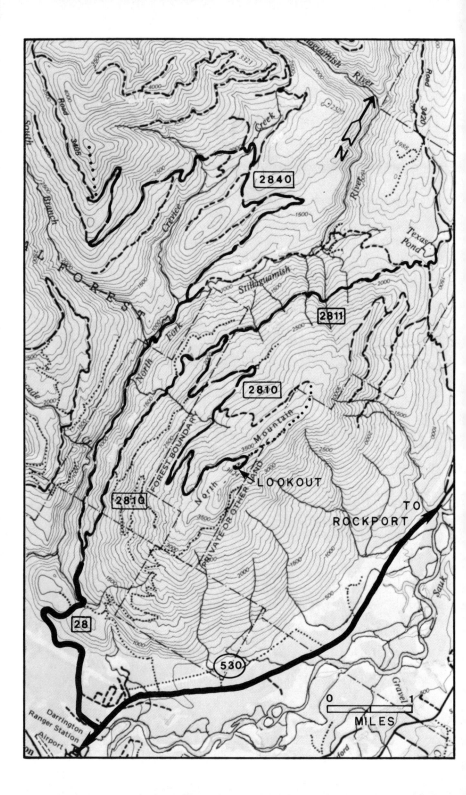

North Mountain Lookout

crowd is not out in force. Ski 3½ miles, gaining 1000 feet, then take a
right and switchback another 6½ miles up to open slopes and a
tremendous viewpoint at the 3956-foot lookout. In winter this is an overnight destination; in March and April, when the road can be driven farther, it's an easy day.

For shorter trips or on days when the machines are marauding, take the
lower left fork at the 1000-foot intersection. The road remains at a near-
constant elevation 4 miles to the crossing of the North Fork Stillaguamish
River. In ¼ mile more the road splits. The left fork, Road 2840, winds 12
miles up to an end on a 4000-foot ridge top. Clearcuts along the way provide a succession of vistas; views from the top are superb.

48 SEGELSEN CREEK ROAD

Skill level: advanced basic
Round trip: up to 24 miles
Skiing time: 2 hours–2 days
Elevation gain: up to 3000 feet
High point: 3431 feet at Deer Creek Pass
Best: January–April
Avalanche potential: low
Map: Green Trails, Darrington

A week could be spent skiing here without covering the whole area, which extends from near rain forest on the valley floor to open ridges 3000 feet above with views out to a formidable lineup of glaciered and snow-clad Cascade giants.

Whitehorse Mountain from Segelsen Creek Road

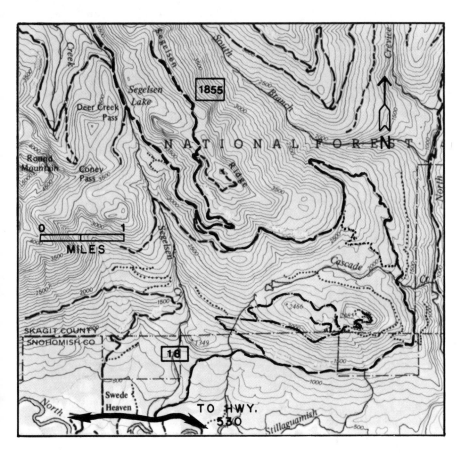

As with all the local roads, Segelsen Creek Road has an extremely variable snowline. Depending on whims of the weather, skiers from January through March may start at the absolute bottom—or 5 miles up. Only the spring skier can reasonably hope to drive more than the first few miles. However, the skiing is fun and the views are good no matter where the capricious snowline is.

Access: Drive Highway 530 east from Arlington 24 miles to the small community of Whitehorse. Just opposite the Whitehorse Mercantile (gas station and store) turn left on Swede Heaven Road for 1.7 miles, crossing the railroad tracks and bridge and passing fields. Go right on Segelsen Creek road No. 18. Trip mileages in the following description start from this intersection (420 feet).

The Tour: The way climbs through a tunnel of moss-covered trees. Ignore all signs proclaiming this to be a private road. The public *does* have

Rainforest on the lower Segelsen Creek Road

legal access here. At 2 miles a spur road heads sharply back left. When the snow level is low, follow this steeply climbing road as far as energy and ambition will take you. Be sure to reach at least one clearcut for views over fields and farms in the valley below and to glacier-carved Whitehorse Mountain filling the horizon beyond. Armed with an up-to-date Green Trails or Forest Service map, ski to the top of bald knolls (the highest is 2685 feet) or design loops on the intertwining spur roads.

The supreme scenery lies higher than the spur road will take you. If possible, therefore, continue on Road 18. Good views start at about 9 miles from Swede Heaven Road and continue to Segelsen Creek Road's high point, Deer Creek Pass (3431 feet) at 12 miles. Be treated to views of innumerable peaks, some of them recognizable favorites like Glacier Peak, White Chuck, Whitehorse, Bedal, and Pugh, plus a host of less famous peaks that appear quite distinguished in their winter whites.

An alternate trip for spring skiers is Segelsen Ridge Road. Take a right fork off Road 18 at 9½ miles (3250 feet) and follow Road 1855 as it climbs steeply 1½ miles to the 4300-foot ridge. Skim along the ridge top for 2 miles of limitless views.

49 PILCHUCK MOUNTAIN

Skill level: intermediate
Round trip: 14 miles
Skiing time: 6 hours–2 days
Elevation gain: 2120 feet

High point: 3120 feet
Best: January–February
Avalanche potential: low
Map: Green Trails, Granite Falls

Pilchuck Mountain once was the scene of bustling winter activity as cars drove bumper to bumper up a winding road 7 miles to ski one of Washington's most challenging downhill runs. Lodge skiers, avoiding the embarrassments of cliff skiing, were once treated to an excellent view across Robe Valley to 6854-foot Three Fingers. Today the lifts and crowds have gone, beaten by poor weather and too many cliffs for beginners. However, the views and an excellent skiing road remain—all the better because nowadays the road after the first 1½ miles is reserved in winter for nonmotorized use. The parking area at the top makes a comfortable and scenic campsite and the once-groomed slope below the old lodge is ideal for a little downhill-telemark practice.

Access: Drive the Mountain Loop Highway 1 mile east of Verlot Ranger Station. Immediately after crossing the South Fork Stillaguamish River, turn right on Pilchuck road No. 42, in midwinter often gated at this point.

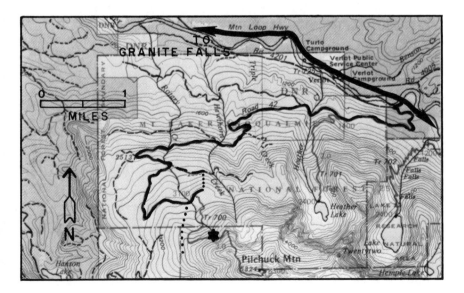

Three Fingers Mountain from the old Pilchuck Mountain downhill ski area

Early- and late-season skiers may be able to drive another 1.5 miles to a second gate, closed all winter, where all motorized vehicles must stop. Park in the Heather Lake Trail parking area (1400 feet).

Intriguing though the lake trail may be, after the first ½ mile it becomes steep and narrow in deep forest, unsuitable for skiing.

The Tour: Pilchuck Road climbs steadily, passing several spurs that offer sidetrips. The two most interesting are just below the 2- and 5-mile markers. Both roads wind through clearcuts with long views north and west. After 5 miles the road levels somewhat as it starts a long switchback that ends 2 scenic miles later at the old ski area.

Skiers wishing to climb higher will find easy access across the old ski slope above the lodge. An old service road begins a short way up the slope on the right side, winds through the trees, and reemerges just below the summit of the first hill. Beyond this point the route is difficult, ascending steep slopes and a short cliff to the top of the old ski area. Ski ascents of 5324-foot Pilchuck should be confined to late spring; avalanche potential on the upper mountain is extreme.

On the return, advanced skiers may short-cut by descending the open slope below the lodge. Near the bottom left a logging spur can be picked up that rejoins the main road just above the 5-mile marker.

50 SCHWEITZER CREEK LOOP

Skill level: intermediate
Round trip: 14 miles
Skiing time: 8 hours
Elevation gain: 1800 feet

High point: 2800 feet
Best: January–February
Avalanche potential: low
Map: Green Trails, Silverton

Day trips, overnight trips, sidetrips, and loop trips—they're all here. Take as much time as you can spare to fully explore this area or plan to come back several times.

Well, that's the good news. The bad news is snowshoers, hikers, dogsleds, three-wheelers, four-wheelers, snowmobiles—they're all here, too. Don't discount the skiing altogether, though. The parade can be entertaining and the skiing, especially during midweek, is very good.

Access: Drive east 11 miles from Granite Falls on the Mountain Loop Highway to the Verlot Ranger Station and then 3.9 miles more to Schweitzer Creek road No. 4020 (1200 feet).

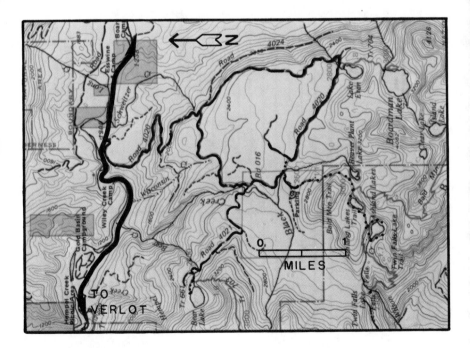

The Tour: The road starts off with an intersection. Stay to the right and climb above the mushy flats on the valley floor. You'll pass several spur roads before reaching the loop portion of the tour at 2¾ miles (2150 feet). There is no best way to do the loop, so please yourself. We will describe it clockwise, going left on Road 4020.

The views are excellent as the road traverses along the edge of a flat-topped ridge overlooking Boardman Creek and Mallardy Ridge. Look for Big Four Mountain as well as Vesper, Sperry Peaks, and Three Fingers. Near 5 miles cross Evan Creek, round a steep switchback, and look for the trail to Lake Evan. The lake is located only a few hundred feet from the road (2751 feet). No nice camping sites exist here, but the trail can be followed another mile to pretty Boardman Lake, located in a rocky cirque. Camping is good but must be reached by crossing a slippery logjam over the outlet stream.

Time exposure of a winter camp

To continue the loop, follow Road 4020 as it levels off at 2800 feet (near mile 6) then descends gently through an open clearcut and heads back into trees (at least there were still trees in 1987). Rounding a bend, the road turns north. Now it is important to watch carefully on the left for a blue diamond or possibly a sign noting where to leave the road on a faint trail. Carefully follow the blue diamonds for ¼ mile to the Ashland Lakes Trail (the trail is actually a road at this point). Time for another choice. To the left (south) you may make a sidetrip to Ashland Lakes. The loop goes right.

For the sidetrip, follow the road down ¼ mile to a creek, then climb to the old trailhead parking area, an excellent winter campsite. From the left-hand side of the parking area the trail heads steeply up an old logging road to a platform and then straight into the brush. Here it levels out for a ½ mile, then climbs another ½ mile to Beaver Plant Lake and good camp-sites (2900 feet). Continue on through dense forest for another ½ mile to the two Ashland Lakes and more campsites.

The loop trip heads north for ¼ mile to an intersection and new trail-head parking. Stay to the left for a short descent to Road 4021 at 7 miles (2400 feet). Here is yet another chance for a sidetrip. Road 4021 may be followed 1¾ miles left to the Bear Lake Trailhead (2600 feet) followed by a ¼-mile trail to the lake and more campsites.

The loop follows Road 4021 to the north, right, contouring along a flat-topped ridge with views of Three Fingers and Mount Pilchuck. At about 8 miles a rolling descent leads back to Road 4020 at 9¼ miles and closes the loop. Descend Road 4020 back to the Mountain Loop Highway at mile 12.

Clearcuts can provide excellent skiing.

51 MALLARDY RIDGE

Skill level: basic
Round trip: 4–12 miles
Skiing time: 2–8 hours
Elevation gain: 2300 feet

High point: 3600 feet
Best: January–February
Avalanche potential: low
Map: Green Trails, Silverton

Three very different types of tours await you around the Mallardy Ridge environs. One nearly level tour leads to bubbling Blackjack Creek. Another tour challenges the steep, open clearcuts where telemarkers can carve graceful turns. The third tour climbs logging roads from the moss-covered valley floor to the windblown winterland of Mallardy Ridge and is just steep enough for a brisk return trip.

Access: Drive east from the Verlot Ranger Station 7.1 miles on the Mountain Loop Highway. Just before the bridge across the South Fork of the Stillaguamish River, Mallardy Ridge road No. 4030 takes off on the right. Park along the side of the highway, out of traffic's way. The elevation is very low here (1300 feet), so make your plans as flexible as the snowline.

The Tour: With luck, skiing will start right at the highway. All three of the tours start together on a fairly level road that crosses Mallardy Creek and makes a quick, steep climb to a broad terrace.

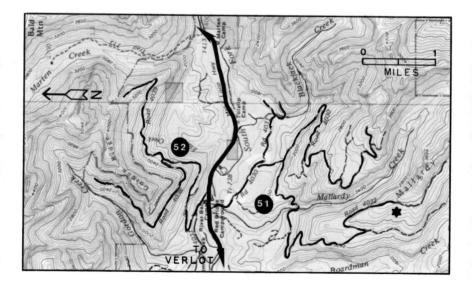

Mallardy Ridge Road

Avoid an important-looking spur on the right and follow the gently rolling terrain to an intersection just before mile 1. The left fork, Road 4031, is the best for novice skiers as it continues along the terrace for another level mile to Blackjack Creek (1440 feet). Here the road divides, offering two short excursions across the creek, both ending in clearcuts. Round trip back to the highway is 4 miles.

Those planning on one of the longer excursions should stay to the right at the intersection of Roads 4030 and 4031 and ski on about ¼ mile to a second major intersection at 1600 feet. The left fork, Road 4030, is for the telemarkers. It climbs rapidly up for the next 4 miles to clearcuts and ends at 3600 feet. When there is enough snow, these north-facing slopes make for excellent skiing and an exhilarating descent.

The third option (the rolling tour up to Mallardy Ridge) goes right, heading toward the Mallardy Ridge Trail on Road 4032. The road climbs for ½ mile, descends to cross Mallardy Creek, and then climbs steeply up to the ridge. Several spots along this road are ideal for a scenic lunch with vistas out over Boardman and Schweitzer creeks. Near 5 miles the road crests the ridge. This is the turnaround point when the snow is unstable. In stable conditions, however, you can follow the road as it crosses a steep, exposed slope before cutting back to the west side of the ridge to reach the Mallardy Ridge trailhead at 6 miles.

52 RED BRIDGE TOUR

Skill level: advanced basic
Round trip: 6 miles
Skiing time: 3 hours
Elevation gain: 2100 feet
High point: 3400 feet

Best: January–February
Avalanche potential: low
Map: Green Trails, Silverton

See map on page 142.

Starting from Red Bridge on the Mountain Loop Highway, this tour climbs from the forested valley floor to clearcuts and ridge-top views. This is a very popular area in the winter so you should expect on a weekend to share your tour with other skiers, hikers, snowshoers, snowmobilers, and people pushing trucks and jeeps out of ditches.

Access: Drive the Mountain Loop Highway 7.1 miles east from the Forest Service Information Center at Verlot. Pass the Mallardy Ridge Road (see Tour 51), and cross the South Fork Stillaguamish River on the Red Bridge. Park just beyond the bridge on the north side of the highway at the beginning of Forest Road 4037 (1300 feet).

The Tour: Take time and a flashlight to explore the old mine in the hillside near the parking area, then ski Road 4037 for ¼ mile along the river. Snow may be scarce here, but worry not, the road soon climbs.

Arriving at the first road junction along the river, take a right on Road 4038 and head uphill through forest and clearcuts. After climbing steadily, the road splits at 1¾ miles (2300 feet). The left fork takes a nearly level traverse into the Gordon Creek drainage, so head right on Road 4039 for views. Note that Mount Pilchuck is already in view, as is the long top of Bald Mountain.

At 2¾ miles the road tops the 3050-foot ridge at an excellent viewpoint and lunch spot overlooking Marten Creek, with Long and Bald mountains leading the eye toward Big Four, Little Chief, Sperry, and Vesper peaks. The road turns abruptly to follow the ridge crest for a final ¼ mile, ending at a safe distance from the rocky avalanche gullies of Gordon Ridge.

Skiers on lower Gordon Ridge

53 DEER CREEK ROAD

Skill level: advanced basic
Round trip: 8½ miles to road-end
Skiing time: 6 hours
Elevation gain: 1500 feet

High point: 3100 feet
Best: January–March
Avalanche potential: low
Map: Green Trails, Silverton

The particular appeal of Deer Creek is that it is one of two areas along the South Fork Stillaguamish River (the other being Mount Pilchuck) reserved for nonmotorized sports. Once past the throngs of enthusiastic snow-players, skiers will find peaceful forest, snow-shrouded clearcuts, and awesome views of rough peaks.

Access: Drive the Mountain Loop Highway east from Verlot Ranger Station 12.1 miles to the end of plowing at Deer Creek road No. 4052 and park alongside the highway (1600 feet).

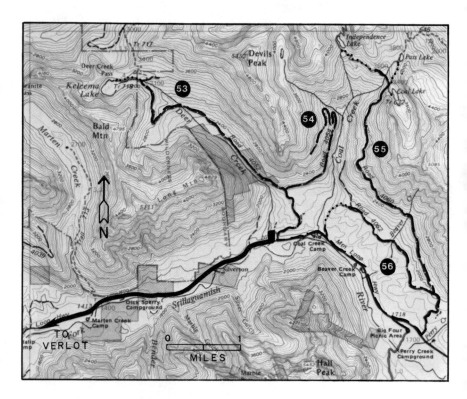

Deer Creek

The Tour: Taking care to dodge exuberant (and sometimes out-of-control) sledders, follow Deer Creek Road steeply uphill through dense second growth to a small knob. In the first ½ mile two spurs branch off; stay left at both. At 1 mile (2000 feet) the Double Eagle Road (see Tour 54) heads east. Continue left on Deer Creek Road, climbing steadily northwest, deeper into the long valley toward Bald Mountain, impressive in its cloak of snow.

Views start at 1¼ miles, however, and improve as you climb. At 2¼ miles, a creek crosses over the road on a specially designed cement bed. Expect to carry your skis across the creek. Shortly after the creek the views expand to include Big Four and the jagged summits of the Monte Cristo group. In a scant ½ mile more the road abruptly turns north, away from Bald Mountain, and ascends a final 1¼ miles to its end in a clearcut just beyond the second crossing of Deer Creek. The return is a long, fun glide.

Near the road-end two trails take off. The upper one, best suited to snowshoers, climbs ½ mile through forest to Deer Creek Pass. The lower one, starting just past the second crossing of Deer Creek, leads a scant ½ mile to Kelcema Lake; it is negotiable by experienced skiers, brave intermediates, and beginners proficient in using tree trunks and branches to slow their descent. The route is not well marked but can be followed to the lake by keeping about 500 feet right of the creek the whole way. On the east shore are several sheltered campsites.

SOUTH FORK STILLAGUAMISH RIVER

54 DOUBLE EAGLE TOUR

Skill level: intermediate
Round trip: 8 miles
Skiing time: 5 hours
Elevation gain: 1500 feet
High point: 3100 feet

Best: January–March
Avalanche potential: low
Map: Green Trails, Silverton

See map on page 146.

The Deer Creek "muscle-powered sports preserve" is a place for the human spirit to run free, unshackled by machinery. Families with children need only sleds and inner tubes to enjoy a winter wonderland more fun than Disneyland. Skiers can enjoy watching the rocketing and screaming kids—and then proceed onward to quiet, peace, and dramatic views of peaks from Monte Cristo to Pilchuck.

Access: Drive to the Deer Creek snow-play area (1600 feet; see Tour 53).

The Tour: Ski Deer Creek Road 1 mile and turn right on Double Eagle Road 4054 which climbs rapidly at first, then settles into a lesser, but steady, ascent. After 1 mile of forest, vistas begin. Look out across the Stillaguamish Valley to Big Four Mountain, its great north face ribboned by avalanche chutes, and to next-door Sperry Peak, and look easterly to peaks of the Monte Cristo group. Across Coal Creek Valley the aftermath of massive clearcutting is revealed in miles of open slopes leading to Coal and Independence lakes.

Upper portion of Double Eagle Road

Double Eagle Road is wide enough at the start for two-way traffic. Higher, the brush closes in, just permitting skiers to sneak through. At 3¾ miles the road drops a bit, then abruptly quits, at a perfect spot to have lunch and soak in the scenery from Monte Cristo to Pilchuck.

The return tends to be rapid and in icy conditions a little tricky. Watch for rabbits, squirrels, and their tracks. Take note of the rocky wall which borders the road in several sections; on warm days a stone or two may be shed.

149

55 COAL LAKE

Skill level: *intermediate*
Round trip: *up to 14½ miles*
Skiing time: *5 hours–2 days*
Elevation gain: *2160 feet*
High point: *3760 feet*

Best: *January–April*
Avalanche potential: *moderate*
Map: *Green Trails, Silverton*

See map on page 146.

The road to Coal Lake does two great things: (1) It escapes the main traffic flow of the Mountain Loop Highway and (2) it leads to fantastic views of peaks from Mount Pilchuck to Big Four Mountain and Sperry

Del Campo Peak from Coal Lake Road

Coal Lake Road

Peak and much more. As everywhere throughout the Stillaguamish Valley, the roar of snow machines echoes, and lonesomeness is not to be expected. A nordic skier with a little adventure in the heart, however, can find a day or more of peace at Coal Lake.

Access: Drive the Mountain Loop Highway east from Silverton to the end of the plowing. Park alongside the road (1600 feet).

The Tour: Ski the Mountain Loop Highway 2½ miles. A short bit beyond the turnoff to Big Four Picnic Area go left at a sign pointing to Coal Lake road No. 4060.

The road climbs gradually in forest that soon thins to open vistas on the Stillaguamish Valley and surrounding peaks. The great north wall of Big Four dominates, but other mountains have their say.

Avalanche hazard is low until about ¾ mile from the lake. Just before the road enters into heavy timber a short, 200-foot open stretch of slopes must be watched. Spot the lake on the right side of the road; there are some very nice campsites.

For further explorations continue on an unmarked path to Pass Lake or Independence Lake.

The run home is gentle but sometimes rapid. It has a few tight corners, so don't get distracted by the view.

56 BIG FOUR LOOP

Mountain Loop Highway

Skill level: basic
Round trip: 5 miles to picnic area
Skiing time: 3 hours
Elevation gain: 180 feet
High point: 1780 feet
Best: January–mid-March
Avalanche potential: none
Map: Green Trails, Silverton

Coal Creek Loop

Skill level: intermediate
Round trip: 6 miles
Skiing time: 4 hours
Elevation gain: 400 feet
High point: 2000 feet
Best: January–mid-March
Avalanche potential: low
Map: Green Trails, Silverton

See map on page 146.

The Mountain Loop Highway makes a splendid tour. The valley bottom is gently rolling; the lush forest, moss-hung trees, snowbound Stillaguamish River, and steep-walled mountains are superbly scenic. A perfect tour? Not quite. Due to the relatively low elevation, the highway provides an easy entry to the wonders of winter and on a fine Sunday half the snow-players in the state pour into the valley. Four-wheelers come in trucks and jeeps to "see how far they can get." Innocent family sedans trustingly follow the ruts, high-center, get stuck, can't turn around, and have to be pulled out by four-wheelers. Snow machines razz through the tangle, dog sleds mush by, snowshoers web, hikers slog. It's a mind-twister as hard as Rubik's Cube to unravel, but not so hot for skiing. For *that* the best time is the middle of the week—and/or immediately after a heavy snowfall that scares out even the jeep heroes. Ah, peace! Ah, the joy of making a single, quiet track through virgin snows in the virgin forest!

In addition to the straight-shot ski run up the highway to Big Four Picnic Area, a traffic-escaping loop can be made via Coal Lake Road. The trip also can be extended up the highway to other scenic objectives.

Access: Drive the Mountain Loop Highway east from Silverton to the end of the plowing. Park along the side of the road (1600 feet).

The Tour: Head east. In ½ mile cross Coal Creek and pass Road 4057, the return leg of the loop trip described below. At 2½ miles is Big Four Picnic Area, in a meadow where a resort hotel was located until 1949 when it burned to the ground. The mountain is still there, 6135-foot Big Four, tall and cold and, when the sun touches it, roaring with avalanches.

A popular winter walk is the 1-mile trail to—or near—the ice caves. Stay well within the trees to be safe from avalanches that pile up the snows in which the ice caves are formed by creeks and winds.

To return via the loop, continue on the highway a bit beyond the picnic

A frozen stream

area and turn left on Coal Lake road No. 4060. In ½ mile pass a fork to the right, and take the first fork to the left, Road 4062. Ski down clearcuts, then over the valley bottom, 2 miles to the road-end. Follow the marked trail through forest to Road 4057. Turn left ¼ mile to return to the highway just above Coal Creek.

When not chopped up by machines, the Mountain Loop Highway makes a good ski trail beyond Big Four to Barlow Pass, 8 miles, except for a short stretch above Perry Creek, which poses an avalanche hazard in unstable conditions.

Another scenic tour is Sunrise Mine Road. At 5 miles turn off the highway on Road 4065, which in 2 miles enters a beautiful cirque. Avalanche potential is high along the mine road and in the cirque.

During years when the snowfall is very low, the Mountain Loop Highway is open to Barlow Pass. In this case the gated Monte Cristo Road offers a scenic 4-mile tour to the old mining town.

57 LAKE ELIZABETH

Skill level: basic
Round trip: 13 miles
Skiing time: 7 hours
Elevation gain: 1930 feet
High point: 2850 feet

Best: January–March
Avalanche potential: low
Maps: Green Trails, Skykomish and
   Mt. Si

How low can you get? Probably not much lower than this tour, which starts at 920 feet. Obviously if you try out new skis here when the snow level is up, you'll lower your spirits. So try this tour when the snow level is low, got it?

The tour follows Money Creek Valley for 6½ miles to a small subalpine lake and a pass boxed in by steep hills. In 1987 the road was gated at the bottom due to a fortuitous washout several miles up. Snowmobiles and other motorized equipment were completely shut out. Unfortunately, due to the mining claims in the area, the road will be repaired in years to come.

Access: Drive Highway 2 east 17.5 miles from Gold Bar or 2.7 miles west from Skykomish. At the Money Creek Campground sign, turn right (south) and follow the Old Cascade Highway for 1 mile before turning right at the Miller River road No. 6410. Go 200 feet and turn right again on Money Creek road No. 6420. Drive straight past the few houses that com-

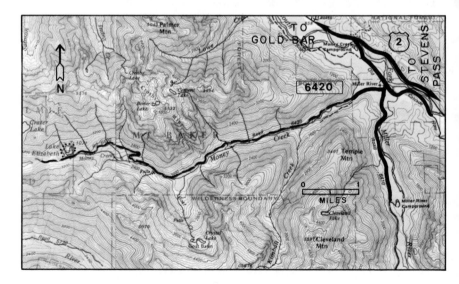

Lake Elizabeth

prise the community of Miller River to the end of the plowed road, or the gate.

The Tour: Ski along the forested valley bottom and enjoy the snow-covered "mushroom rocks" in the creek bed, the snow-laced trees, and streamers of ice dripping from rock walls. Views are few—Temple, Lennox, and Crosby mountains enclose the valley on both sides. At 4 miles the valley opens and Goat Creek merges from the south. The valley then bends to the northwest, enters a narrow gorge (1900 feet), and the road's steepness increases. The banks are steep-sided here and subject to rock slides. After 5 miles the road makes a short switchback and gives views of the snowy slopes on Lennox Mountain. At 6½ miles the road passes Lake Elizabeth (2850 feet). The road continues another ¼ mile, crosses over a narrow pass into the Tolt Valley, and dead-ends.

SKYKOMISH RIVER

58 MILLER RIVER

Skill level: basic
Round trip: 4–15 miles
Skiing time: 3 hours–2 days
Elevation gain: up to 2100 feet
High point: 3058 feet at Lake
  Dorothy

Best: January–March
Avalanche potential: low
Map: Green Trails, Skykomish

Moss-draped trees, rivers, waterfalls, and spots for viewing mountain goats in their winter quarters on valley cliffs. The route begins on a logging road through rain forest-like vegetation with looks up to 5591-foot Cascade Mountain. Advanced skiers may continue on a 1½-mile trail into the Alpine Lakes Wilderness to Lake Dorothy, with views of snow-covered Big Snow Mountain.

Access: Drive Highway 2 to the Money Creek Campground sign (located at the west entrance of the tunnel, 2.7 miles west of Skykomish). Turn south on the Old Cascade Highway for 1 mile then go right on Miller River Road. In 100 feet pass Money Creek Road on the right (see Tour 57) and continue straight to the end of the plowed road at Miller River Campground (1040 feet).

The Tour: From the campground intersection go right and glide along beside Miller River in dense timber 1½ miles. When the West Fork Road branches off right, keep left and cross the West Fork Miller River. At ⅛ mile beyond the bridge is the first of the two goat-viewing spots; from a turnout on the left side of the road gaze across the valley, watching the

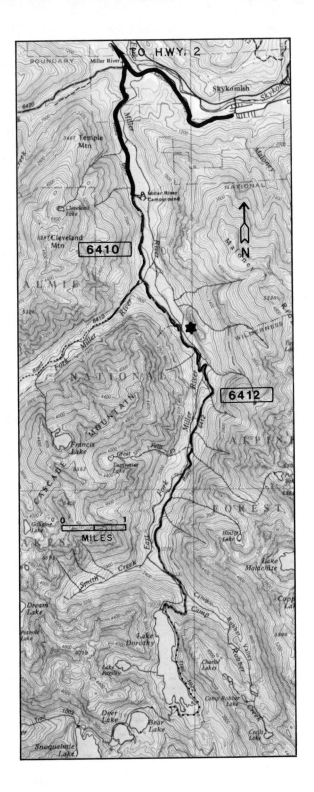

Lake Dorothy Trail after an early-season melt

cliffs for little snow patches that walk. In times of high avalanche potential, make this the turnaround, avoiding a dangerous chute 1 mile ahead.

The second goat-viewing spot is the East Fork Miller River Bridge at 3 miles. The road ends in 2½ miles more, 6 miles from Miller River Campground, at the Lake Dorothy Trailhead (2100 feet). The trail takes off from the far right end of the parking area and is so wide that it is fairly easy to follow even when deep in snow.

At 1 mile (2480 feet), the trail crosses Camp Robber Creek—just as it joins the Miller River—on a wide bridge overlooking a pretty series of cascades. From here head straight up into a basin, contour its headwall, and climb steadily northwest to the lake outlet (3058 feet).

The lakeshore trail offers 2 more miles of easy touring. Camping is good all along the east shore.

59 EAGLE CREEK

Skill level: advanced basic
Round trip: up to 10 miles
Skiing time: 4 hours
Elevation gain: up to 3100 feet
High point: 4000 feet

Best: mid-December–March
Avalanche potential: moderate
Maps: Green Trails, Skykomish and
  Monte Cristo

Eagle Creek is an easy access area with miles of roads to explore, open hillsides for cross-country descents, and endless views which keep you coming back for more. The tour lies on the edge of the proposed Eagle Rock Roadless Area and two easy overnight trips into the backcountry may be started from the logging roads.

Access: Drive Highway 2 from Skykomish for .7 mile east of the Chevron station. Turn left on Beckler River road No. 65, (880 feet). When snowfall has been heavy this is the starting point for skiing. If the road is drivable, continue on .8 mile to the first major intersection and go left on Road 6510. Skiing directions start here.

Eagle Creek, Beckler River valleys

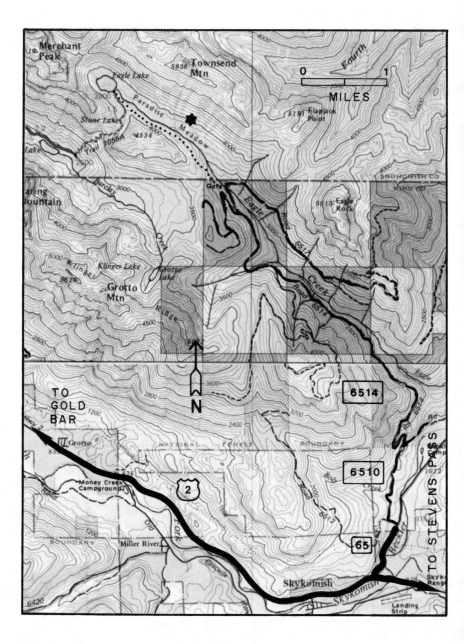

The Tour: Ski Road 6510 up a short incline to a large intersection. The main road goes right, while on the left, Road 6512 climbs for 2 miles to a broad logging platform with an outstanding view over the town of Skykomish and the snowcapped peaks of the Alpine Lakes Wilderness.

Remaining on Road 6510, traverse north for the next mile, tunneling through a dense canopy of forest and brush. At the end of the first mile the road divides (1200 feet). Go left on Road 6514 (Road 6510 descends back to Beckler River and, when not rutted by trucks, makes a good tour for first-time skiers).

Road 6514 climbs rapidly in a short series of steep switchbacks that are difficult to descend when icy. There is one viewpoint of Mounts Hinman and Daniels along this section that makes the climb worthwhile.

At 1¾ miles the road widens to a large platform, then turns northwest into the Eagle Creek drainage. When the snow is unstable, this is the best turnaround point. Beyond, the beautiful Eagle Creek Valley has been mercilessly logged from the valley floor to the ridge tops several thousand feet above. Expect sliding, especially at the natural hillside drainage points. Stay out of the Eagle Creek Valley during and for several days after any rain or wet snowstorm.

Views increase as you head up the valley. Eagle Rock (5615 feet) is the first peak to come into view, followed by the forested slopes of Flapjack Point and the long, open summit of Townsend Mountain. At 3½ miles awaits a major junction. Continue straight ahead on Road 6514 (to the left, Road 6516 climbs up and over potentially avalanche-prone slopes to Klinger Ridge [4400 feet] and excellent views).

At 4 miles the road crosses a small creek with views of Grotto Mountain. The road divides again at 4¾ miles. Go left, still on Road 6514, and switchback up to the ridge top. The road divides yet again in ¼ mile; go right to the ridge top and enjoy the views that start with the glacier-cut valley between Baring and Merchant peaks, extend down Barclay Creek to the South Fork of the Skykomish River, and end in the pinkish haze of the Puget Sound Basin.

Two backcountry trips start from the junction at 4¾ miles. The first trip is to 3888-foot Eagle Lake. Go right at 4¾ miles on Road 6517 for ⅛ mile to cross Eagle Creek, then leave the road. Ski up the valley for 2 miles to the lake, following the creek. This trip can only be done when adequate snow covers the dense brush. Stay on the south side of the creek as much as possible—the steep slopes descending from Townsend Mountain on the north are very avalanche-prone. The safest camping is south of Eagle Lake at little Stone Lake. Eagle Lake may also be approached from the end of Road 6514 by following the ridge west.

The objectives of the second backcountry trip are two small lakes between Flapjack Point and Townsend Mountain. Climbing skins are necessary for this tour. From the intersection at 4¾ miles, ski to the right on Road 6517. Cross Eagle Creek and then enter the forest, heading northeast toward a 4680-foot saddle between Flapjack and Townsend. The first lake lies directly north of the saddle at 4400 feet. The second lake is to the west on a small bench at 4860 feet.

60 TONGA RIDGE AND FOSS RIVER

Tonga Ridge

Skill level: intermediate
Round trip: 5 miles
Skiing time: 3 hours
Elevation gain: 1100 feet
High point: 4800 feet
Best: November and April
Avalanche potential: moderate
Map: Green Trails, Skykomish

Foss River

Skill level: basic
Round trip: 2–20 miles
Skiing time: 1 hour–2 days
Elevation gain: 100–2960 feet
High point: 4320 feet
Best: mid-December–April
Avalanche potential: low
Maps: Green Trails, Skykomish and
Stevens Pass

From the first snowfall of late autumn to those rocky last runs of early summer, and in all the months in between, there are Foss River trails to engage skiers at any level. Each trail has a special scenic character, whether of serene valley floor or icy-craggy Alpine Lakes Wilderness.

Access: Drive Highway 2 east 1.8 miles from Skykomish and turn right on Foss River road No. 68. At 1.2 miles turn right again. At 2.5 miles pass under a railroad trestle to the winter parking area (1280 feet).

Snow-covered forest

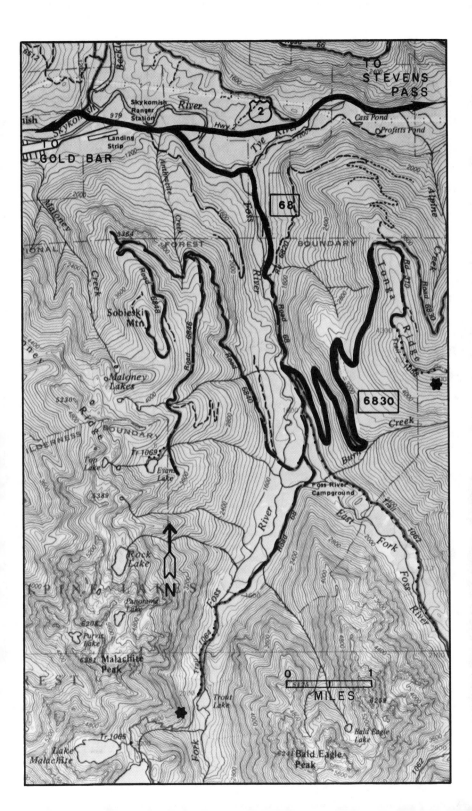

Mount Baring, Merchant and Gunn peaks from Tonga Ridge

Tonga Ridge: In early and late season the best skiing is on Tonga Ridge, which offers numerous viewpoints of Mount Baring, Glacier Peak, and the ramparts leading to Mount Daniel. The route is not recommended in midwinter due to (1) snowmobilers and (2) avalanches which somehow fail to eliminate (1). Though basic skiers may be able to carry skis up and down the steep forest trail, the trip is not recommended for those below the intermediate level.

From the winter parking area continue up Foss River Road to 3.6 miles from Highway 2 and turn left on Tonga Ridge Road No. 6830. At 13.6 miles (3880 feet), the road's highest point, find a spur on the right, signed "Tonga Ridge." Ski (or drive, as the case may be) 1½ miles up the steep spur to its end and the trailhead (4400 feet).

The trail begins by abruptly gaining 200 feet up the edge of a clearcut, then climbs a mile of forest to meadows of the Alpine Lakes Wilderness. The upsy-downsy way contours another 2 miles around Sawyer Mountain to Sawyer Pass (4800 feet).

Foss River: Except for the first mile, Foss River Road is reserved for nonmotorized sports and most snowmobilers abide by the rule. The Forest Service additionally has marked two ski trails into the Alpine Lakes Wilderness. The road therefore can be heartily recommended for an afternoon or overnight tour during the loudest months of winter.

From the 1280-foot parking area ski the long, flattish mile to the Tonga Ridge Road, passing a rock wall that may display a fantasy of icicles. At the junction go straight ahead.

At 2 miles pass the East Fork Foss River Trail; this is a very nice sidetrip for intermediate skiers heading 5 miles up a U-shaped valley. Stop when the trail turns west, crossing the East Fork Foss River to start its 3-mile climb up to Necklace Valley. This final section has a high avalanche potential throughout the winter.

At 2½ miles on Foss River Road a spur leads to West Fork Foss River Trail, another sidetrip which offers 3 miles of skiing before becoming avalanche-prone. There are no views.

The Foss River Road crosses the West Fork of the Foss River Bridge at 2¾ miles, then starts its long climb up steep open slopes to Maloney Ridge. The bridge is a good turnaround point when conditions are unstable. A quarter-mile beyond the bridge the road divides; stay left and continue climbing.

At 6½ miles keep right at a major junction, and continue to the radio tower at 9 miles (3364 feet). The views extend up and down the Skykomish River to Mount Index, Mount Baring, and Glacier Peak. To see Mount Daniel and Mount Hinman follow the road to Sobieski Mountain at 12 miles (4400 feet).

61 BECKLER PEAK ROAD

Skill level: intermediate
Round trip: 3–14 miles
Skiing time: 2 hours–2 days
Elevation gain: up to 2900 feet
High point: 4200 feet

Best: March–April
Avalanche potential: low
Maps: Green Trails, Skykomish and
  Stevens Pass

Views and more views. Ski high above the Beckler River to overlooks down the South Fork Skykomish River and up Money Creek. Continuing up the road, gaze southward over the Foss River to a multitude of peaks in the Alpine Lakes Wilderness. Though called the Beckler Peak Road, loggers have extended it on a long, nearly level traverse east to Alpine Baldy, where it ends at about 4200 feet. At 1½, 2, and 3 miles are excellent views and rewarding turnarounds.

The Beckler Peak Road is a designated snowmobile trail, but its relatively short length and lack of midwinter parking generally leave it free from machine hassle. Skiers have the same parking problems as snowmobilers. The only winter space currently available is along the side of Highway 2, where parking is allowed unless a snowplow wishes to clear the area, a frequent occurrence. The best idea is to wait until spring, when the low elevations melt out, leaving ample parking and shorter access to the high viewpoints.

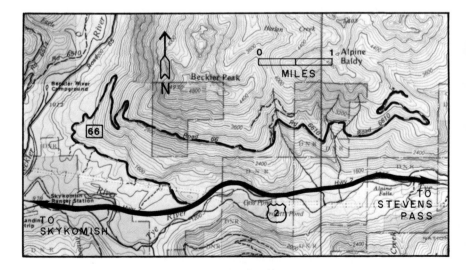

Skykomish River Valley from Beckler Peak Road

Access: Drive Highway 2 east of Skykomish 3.5 miles and turn left (north) on Beckler Peak road No. 66. Drive 2 miles, crossing under powerlines, then northeast around the base of the peak to the beginning of this trip (1240 feet).

The Tour: Walk or drive to the snowline, following the switchbacking road as it climbs briskly through a junglelike tangle of timber, then out into clearcuts. The first viewpoint is at 1½ miles (2200 feet). From a narrow window at midswitchback, look southwest to much-logged Eagle Creek and farther south to white peaks above Money Creek.

Skiing on through the forest, listen for the reverberating sound of male grouse drumming for a mate. At 2 miles is a second viewpoint, perched on the corner of an open switchback. Look north for miles up the Beckler River toward Jack Pass and over innumerable peaks made mighty by their snow coverings. The third viewpoint is at 3 miles (2900 feet) just as the road levels off for its long traverse to Alpine Baldy. Cliffs above prevent ski ascents of 4950-foot Beckler Peak. Below and to the south are Tye and Foss rivers, Tonga Ridge, Maloney microwave tower, Sobieski Mountain, and beyond them, Mount Hinman and Mount Daniels.

Past the third viewpoint the road traverses, losing 120 feet in 1½ miles, then regaining it on Alpine Baldy. Views extend over Deception and Martin creeks to Windy Mountain. From the road-end (4200 feet) an abandoned spur road may be followed up a shoulder to the 4400-foot level on Alpine Baldy. Skiers with advanced level skills may continue up open slopes to the summit at 5200 feet.

Heather Ridge

62 HEATHER RIDGE

Skill level: advanced
Round trip: 4 miles
Skiing time: 3 hours
Elevation gain: 1200 feet
High point: 5200 feet

Best: January–March
Avalanche potential: low
Maps: Green Trails, Stevens Pass
*   and Benchmark Mtn.*

Years before skinny skis, refugees from the mobs at the Stevens Pass Ski Area were fleeing across the highway to untracked slopes of Heather Ridge (sometimes called Skyline Ridge). Though the long, south-facing ascent rarely offered the far-famed "Stevens powder," and explorers were burdened by heavy mountaineering outfits, they returned time and time

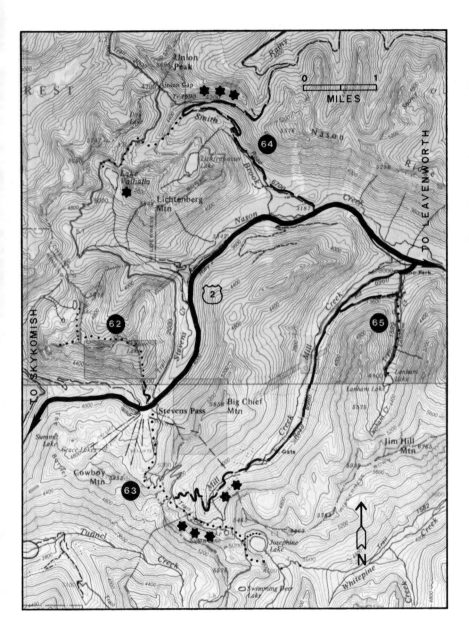

again. Nowadays Heather Ridge is an extremely popular tour for advanced skiers. The reason is the same now as it was then—views over miles and miles of white-topped peaks.

Access: Drive Highway 2 to the summit of Stevens Pass and park on the north side in the downhill lot (4050 feet).

The Tour: Scramble up the snowbank behind the service buildings and follow a cat road to the left. Pass a cluster of vacation cottages on the right and follow an old road through the trees to a telephone relay station at the foot of the open slopes.

To the right of the building a primitive road, obscured by snow, heads steeply up; climbing skins are very helpful. A quarter of the way to the ridge top the road fades away somewhere under the snow. Switchback onward; in unstable conditions stay to the left (west) side of the hill.

At 4900 feet, by a radio relay shed, the hard climbing ends and Mount Hinman and Mount Daniel come in view. However, the really big picture awaits above. Ski northwest just below the heavy timber, then turn uphill in thinning forest to the snow plain of Skyline Lake (5092 feet). Continue to the base of a rock knob on the ridge crest. Unless equipped with ice ax, do not try for the top; be satisfied with the superb view from the saddle including Glacier Peak to the north and Mount Stuart to the southeast.

Warm up for the steep descent by trying some of the short slopes around Skyline Lake, or climb northwest from the lake, over a ridge to a forested bowl for some powder runs.

SKYKOMISH RIVER

63 JOSEPHINE LAKE

Skill level: advanced
Round trip: 7 miles
Skiing time: 4 hours
Elevation gain: 1500 feet
High point: 5300 feet

Best: January–February
Avalanche potential: high
Map: Green Trails, Stevens Pass

See map on page 169.

Excellent powder bowls and outstanding views turn this short tour to Josephine Lake into an all-day affair. You should plan an early start, not only to be sure you have enough time to ski all the bowls, but also to allow time to ski up through the Stevens Pass Ski Area before the lifts start running (that means before 9 A.M. on weekends).

There is a high potential for avalanches on this tour, so ski to Josephine Lake when the snow conditions are very stable and carry full backcountry

Scenery along the Josephine Lake ski route

equipment including shovels, avalanche beacons, climbing skins, and a good map.

Access: Drive Highway 2 to the summit of Stevens Pass and park in the ski area parking lot (4050 feet).

The Tour: Walk up to the lodge and then ski south through the ski area, keeping well out of the way of downhill skiers. Ski below Big Chief chairlift, then up the gentle slopes of the beginning and intermediate runs, past the Tye Mill chairlift, and then climb steeply uphill, following the ski run to the ridge crest (5200 feet).

At the top, ski right. When the ridge starts climbing descend east on a groomed slope or ski down through the trees to the powerline clearing at the upper end of Mill Creek (5000 feet). (Do not follow the groomed run as it turns north to the base chairlift on the backside of Big Chief.) Continue down to the northeast, dropping another 200 feet in elevation, then ski into the trees on the east side of the powerlines.

Follow the sloping bench east, keeping well below the cliffs on the right. Stay low, using the protective cover of the trees when possible. (The north-facing slopes between the cliffs and trees are avalanche-prone and extremely hazardous after any heavy snowfall and in the spring when warmed by the sun.) Despite all precautions there are still a couple of hazardous slopes, easy to pick out because the trees on them never grow more than ten feet tall.

Near the end of the sloping bench is a thick band of trees. Using them for cover, climb up to tiny Lake Susan Jane (4640 feet). Ski around the north side of the lake and at the far (east) end head up the right-hand side of an open slope. At the upper end of the slope follow a stream through the trees to a small open bench (4900 feet). Ski across the bench, then climb left to an upper bench overlooking Josephine Lake. Stop well before the edge of the trees; there is a band of cliffs between you and the lake. Plan to enjoy a long lunch here, gazing over the lake to the southeast where the snow-covered Bulls Tooth overshadows its neighbors.

To reach the lake, ski left through the trees until you are beyond the cliffs, then telemark the 400 feet down to the lake. When the snow is good be sure to save enough time to ski the open bowls above the lake.

64 SMITH BROOK AND LAKE VALHALLA

Smith Brook

Skill level: advanced basic
Round trip: 4 miles
Skiing time: 2 hours
Elevation gain: 800 feet
High point: 4000 feet
Best: January–March
Avalanche potential: low
Map: Green Trails, Benchmark Mtn.

Lake Valhalla

Skill level: advanced
Round trip: 7½ miles
Skiing time: 4 hours
Elevation gain: 1900 feet
High point: 5100 feet
Best: January–April
Avalanche potential: high
Map: Green Trails, Benchmark Mtn.

See map on page 169.

Many of us frequently hear that the Smith Brook Road is a fine tour, but it is time that someone came out of the closet and told you the truth about this one. In actuality the road is an extremely dangerous tour because of

View south over snow-covered Lake Valhalla

the tons of sliding snow that race across it at frighteningly frequent intervals.

To put it plainly, Smith Brook Road is highly prone to avalanches beyond the 2-mile point. Steep, rocky walls 1000 feet above the road shed snow daily, in all kinds of weather. This snow sweeps an unobstructed path down the open hillsides, completely covering the road below, as well as any unfortunate skiers who happen to be at the wrong place at the wrong time.

Now that we've got your attention (i.e., got you scared), we'll tell you about two tours along this road that, if skied with caution, can be skied safely. The first follows the road along the safe section of Smith Brook. This short trip offers side roads to explore and sweeping open slopes of a clearcut to practice telemarking. The long tour leads to Lake Valhalla; it involves routefinding and avoiding several potential avalanche areas to reach the heavenly slopes around and above the lake. Consider this tour only when the snow pack is stable.

Access: Smith Brook Road lies 4.7 miles east of Stevens Pass on a divided section of Highway 2. If approaching from the west it is necessary to drive 6 miles beyond Stevens Pass. Take the Mill Creek U-turn and drive 1.2 miles back toward the pass to the parking area, located .2 mile east of Smith Brook Road.

The Tour: Access to Smith Brook Road (3200 feet) starts with a ¼-mile walk up the highway (or ski along the edge if the snow is clean). The road climbs gently through trees and clearcuts, passing one side road on the right. At 1¾ miles the road makes a broad switchback in a large clearcut before reentering the trees. This is the turnaround point for those skiers who are not heading on to Valhalla.

Advanced skiers, continuing on, should ski up the road, passing a couple of avalanche gullies. When there is enough snow look for a crossing of Smith Brook and ski up the opposite side, because after the gullies the road crosses under a large, very open, and very active avalanche slope. Beyond this slope the road switchbacks. Continue straight off the road, following Smith Brook into an open meadow (4000 feet). Ski across the meadow and into the trees beyond. About 400 to 500 feet beyond the meadow, turn left and ski to the hillside.

Climb up and to the right, staying on the south side of Smith Brook on rolling slopes. At about 4500 feet and forest cover thins. Ahead is an avalanche-prone hillside on the flank of avalanche-prone Lichtenberg Mountain; swing to the right and continue climbing to an open bowl.

Looking straight ahead, southwest, is a saddle. That is the goal. To reach it ski to the northwest, then head southwest up and across a hillside cut by deep gullies. The saddle is reached at 5100 feet, 3½ miles from Highway 2.

Lake Valhalla lies 400 feet below the saddle. To ski the lake, head down steeply to the right from the saddle; slopes to the left tend to avalanche. If the climb back out from the lake is too intimidating, try heading up to the top of the 5700-foot knob above the saddle for some exhilarating skiing down lightly timbered slopes instead.

65 MILL CREEK

Mill Creek Road

Skill level: basic
Round trip: 8 miles to road-end
Skiing time: 5 hours
Elevation gain: 500 feet
High point: 3500 feet
Best: December–March
Avalanche potential: low
Maps: Green Trails, Benchmark
  Mtn. and Stevens Pass

Lanham Lake

Skill level: advanced
Round trip: 3½ miles
Skiing time: 4 hours
Elevation gain: 1200 feet
High point: 4200 feet
Best: December–March
Avalanche potential: none
Map: Green Trails, Benchmark
  Mtn.

See map on page 169.

Mill Creek offers a sort of valley tour unusual for the Cascades, not through deep forest but out in the open with broad vistas of surrounding peaks. Skiers of all levels find the scene uniquely appealing. Unfortunately, so do the snowmobilers. The advanced skier can escape them on a challenging ascent to Lanham Lake.

Note: The fate of this popular tour is uncertain. Mill Creek may be developed in 1989 as a cross-country skier area with a lodge and groomed trails. There are no plans at this time to keep any public parking here. Mill Creek will still be an excellent area for skiing (if you do not mind paying a fee).

If you would like to see public parking at Mill Creek preserved, write the District Ranger and let him know. The address is: Lake Wenatchee Ranger District, Star Route, Box 109, Leavenworth, WA 98826.

Access: Drive Highway 2 east 5.8 miles beyond Stevens Pass to the Sno-Park (2800 feet) on the eastbound lane; an access road gives entry from the westbound lane.

The Tour: Ski up Mill Creek Road, which climbs moderately for 1½ miles, then levels in the wide-open spaces with unlimited views and roaming—and machinery. Follow powerlines the next 2½ miles, passing many picnic spots. The tour ends at the base of the new Stevens Pass chair lift.

From the road-end, 4 miles from the Sno-Park, ambitious skiers, during stable conditions, can follow powerlines 1200 feet up to the Pacific Crest Trail and proceed either north to Stevens Pass Ski Area or south to Lake Susan Jane and Josephine Lake (see Tour 63).

To escape man's trammeling and find peace, beauty, and excellent skiing, aim for Lanham Lake. Leave the valley road on the first spur to the left; at about 1 mile from the Sno-Park it leads up and back to the power-

Lanham Lake and Jim Hill Mountain

lines. Ski along these until the slope drops off just above Lanham Creek, and turn uphill into the trees. Once away from the buzzing and humming of the powerlines (one wonders what the electricity is doing to one's blood, and bones, and brains), cross several old logging roads. Keep left, staying within 500 feet of the creek, traversing open meadows where the works of man are out of sight, hearing, and mind. The valley narrows, the walls close in, and a scant ½ mile of steep climbing leads to Lanham Lake (4143 feet). Nestled in the trees, the serenely frozen lake offers many fine picnic and camp spots with safe views up to icicled ramparts of 6765-foot Jim Hill Mountain.

66 COULTER SKI TRAIL

Skill level: advanced
Round trip: 13 miles to road-end
Skiing time: 6 hours
Elevation gain: 2800 feet
High point: 5000 feet

Best: March–April
Avalanche potential: low
Maps: Green Trails, Wenatchee
Lake and Chiwaukum Mtns.

The Coulter Ski Trail gives access to several days of excellent skiing in the Chiwaukum Mountains. Open, rolling slopes and forested ridges often covered with deep powder, heart-catching vantage points with almost daily sunbreaks, and miles of marked ski trails are just some of the attractions.

The approach is long and requires careful navigation through a complex system of logging roads. There are two good ways. The first is to follow the Coulter Ski Trail marked and maintained by the Starks, owner-operators of the Scottish Lakes cross-country ski resort, but freely open

Overlooking the Coulter and Nason Creek valleys

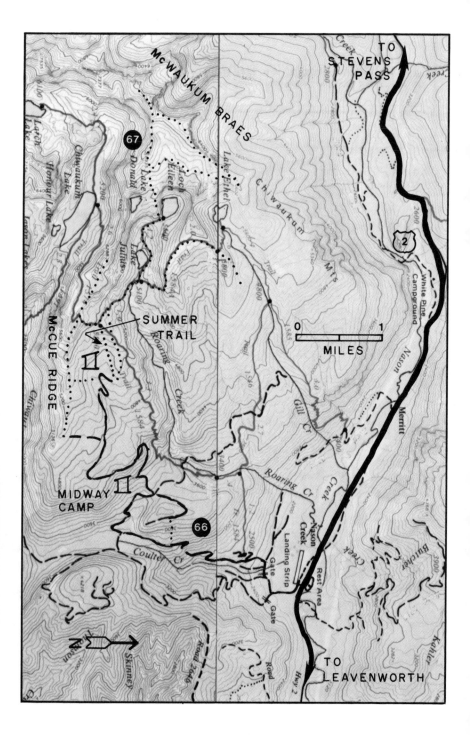

to everyone. The second choice, many say the first, is to ride the Starks' snow-cat—or at least send the packs on it—to their 5000-foot Nomad Ski Camp, saving time and energy for the better skiing above. Visitors may even leave their tents at home and stay in the camp's heated tent cabins. For further information contact Bill and Peg Stark, P.O. Box 303, Leavenworth, Washington 98826.

Access: Drive Highway 2 east of Stevens Pass 17 miles. Just opposite the Rest Area, closed in winter, turn off the highway onto the Coulter Creek road system (2200 feet).

This area is privately owned. The plowing is privately paid for and parking is limited. Please do not block other cars or driveways. Unless a Sno-Park can be established (maybe in the Rest Area), during heavy snow be prepared to park as far away as Leavenworth and hitchhike back.

The Tour: Starting from the railroad tracks, walk the first ¼ mile to a signed junction and turn right on the Coulter Ski Trail. Another ¼ mile brings a left turn at a large Y (2300 feet). As the way climbs, stay left, then go right at the next two intersections. At 1¾ miles enter the base of a clearcut. Ascend to the left, avoiding the cliffs. After gaining 200 feet, head up the clearcut, aiming for the upper right side. Crest the top of a ridge (3900 feet) to find a road and tremendous views west to the Chiwaukums and east to Nason Ridge. Bear left, losing a few hundred feet, to a three-way intersection at 3 miles.

Turn up, following the cat tracks past Starks' Midway Camp and marked ski trails. At 6½ miles, 5000 feet, is Nomad Ski Camp, the end of the Coulter Ski Trail but just the start of the good skiing. Either stay with the Starks or at one of the many excellent campsites to be found in the forest beyond and spend several days exploring this vast skiers' paradise.

67 CHIWAUKUM MOUNTAINS (SCOTTISH LAKES)

Skill level: advanced
Over 20 miles of trails
Skiing time: 1–5 days
Elevation gain: 100–1500 feet
High point: 7000 feet

Best: January–mid-May
Avalanche potential: low
Maps: Green Trails, Wenatchee
    Lake and Chiwaukum Mtns.

See map on page 178.

Miles of open hills, forested ridge tops, checkerboard meadows, and frozen lakes combine to offer some of the most exhilarating skiing in the Cascades. There are marked ski trails and untouched wilderness, short forest loops and long high-country treks in the Scottish Lakes area of the Chiwaukum Mountains.

Access: On Highway 2 between Stevens Pass and Leavenworth, just opposite the Rest Area, find a small road. Only a very few feet along a logging road are available for parking, and skiers in midwinter must be prepared to cope with this problem.

The Tour: Getting into the area requires at least one day. Either ski up the Coulter Ski Trail or make reservations with the Starks (see Tour 66) for snow-cat transport to their Nomad Ski Camp at 5000 feet. If not staying at Nomad Camp, follow the ridge toward Lake Julius and choose from among the numerous campsites along the ridge, the Roaring Creek valley below, or at Loch Eileen. The Starks have laid out and marked a number of trails beginning at Nomad Camp for all degrees of skill and energy.

Serious backcountry skiers will be unable to resist the formidable all-day trip up the McWaukum Braes. From the end of the Coulter Ski Trail ski the Summer Trail along the ridge above Roaring Creek for 1½ miles, then descend to the valley ½ mile below Lake Julius. Head east up the valley, passing Lake Julius to the north. Shortly beyond the lake follow the valley as it makes an abrupt turn to the north. Climb 500 feet in 1 mile to Loch Eileen.

Above Loch Eileen, head east, climbing steeply. This short section has the only avalanche potential in the area and should not be crossed in unstable conditions. At the top of the narrow ledge, go right, skiing above 5900-foot Lake Donald. From here, the skiing is open to the top of any of the three braes.

McCue Ridge is another excellent run. The trip through forest and meadows is marked for the whole 2½ miles of ridge crest and along several of the access trails. It can be skied in all weather conditions but is best on a sunny day when views from a 6258-foot viewpoint extend for miles over the whole Chiwaukum Range.

Lake Julius below the McWaukum Braes

68 LAKE WENATCHEE STATE PARK

Skill level: basic
Round trip: up to 13 miles
Skiing time: 1–6 hours
Elevation gain: up to 430 feet

High point: 2300 feet
Best: January–February
Avalanche potential: none
Map: Green Trails, Plain

From the silent forests to lake waters enlivened by reflections of snow-covered Nason, Wenatchee, and Poe ridges, the rolling terrain around the south entrance to Lake Wenatchee State Park is a mecca for skiers from around the entire state. Especially appealing is the fact that snow-mobiles, which "own" the rest of the area including the north section of the park, are not allowed here.

Access: Drive Highway 2 east 19 miles from Stevens Pass and at Coles Corner turn left on Highway 207 for 3.6 miles. Turn left again at the south entrance to Lake Wenatchee State Park, cross Nason Creek, then stay right as the road splits. Drive to the Sno-Park (1900 feet).

The Tour: The park staff has developed six loops which wind and inter-twine in the limited area of the park. The loops vary in length from 1.5 miles to 6 miles and are all carefully maintained and beautifully groomed.

The Lake Shore Loop is the most scenic. The loop trail follows the shore around the west end of Lake Wenatchee and in good weather Poe Ridge and Dirtyface Peak cast gleaming white reflections on the blue lake

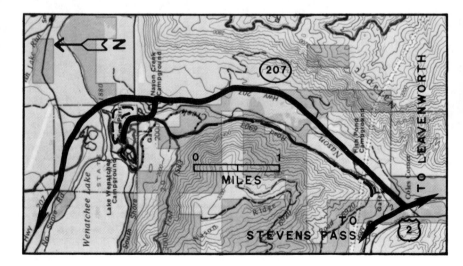

Dirtyface Peak and Lake Wenatchee

waters. River View Loop runs along the edge of the Wenatchee River, Camp Loop takes you on a tour of snow-covered campsites, while the Backwoods Loop leads you through the forest between the upper and lower levels of the park. Nason Creek Loop offers a chance to do some climbing on road and trail, while the Kaller Creek Loop is the objective for long-distance skiers.

Other than the Nason Creek Loop, all trails are as fun for a first-time skier as for an experienced one, except when they are icy. When the roads and trails freeze up solid, beginners should stick to the Lake Shore and Camp loops.

No matter which trail you ski on, take time to look for the tracks of rabbits, birds, and small rodents as well as those of the coyotes and local dogs that pursue them.

69 CHIWAWA SNO-PARK

Skill level: basic
Round trip: up to 15 miles
Skiing time: 2–8 hours
Elevation gain: up to 680 feet

High point: 2590 feet
Best: January–February
Avalanche potential: none
Map: Green Trails, Plain

There are three "Skier Only" trails at the Chiwawa Sno-Park offering a wide variety of scenery and terrain. You may choose to skim along the banks of the Wenatchee River, wander through open forest paralleling a set of coyote tracks, or climb steeply to a pleasant ridge top with viewpoints overlooking the Wenatchee River and the broad Plain Valley.

Access: Drive Highway 2 east 19 miles from Stevens Pass and turn left on Highway 207 at Coles Corner for 4.6 miles. Cross the Wenatchee River, then go right at a Y on the Chiwawa Loop Road for 1.5 miles to the Chiwawa Sno-Park (1970 feet).

The Tour: There is a large information board at the Sno-Park with a map of the ski trails (three) and the snowmobile trails (endless) to help you orient yourself before starting out on one of the following trails.

Squirrel Run Trail is a 4-mile round trip and the easiest of the three trails to ski. The trail starts from the southwest corner of the Sno-Park

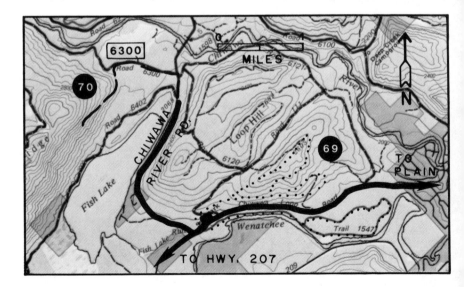

See and Ski Trail, paralleling the Chiwawa River

and climbs gradually on a wide logging road. In ¼ mile cross a groomed snowmobile trail. At ½ mile cross a second snowmobile trail and then head steeply uphill on a trail, leaving the machines behind. At ¾ mile the Flying Loop Trail branches off to the left and Squirrel Run levels off for a gently rolling traverse through the forest. At 1¾ miles the trail starts a ½-mile loop that gently turns you back the way you came.

The See and Ski Trail starts across the road from the Sno-Park. This tour is 6 miles long and the most scenic of the three trails. The trail rolls through the forest for 1½ miles, then starts a loop which sweeps along the edge of the Wenatchee River before heading back to the start on a series of abandoned logging roads. When the snow is soft this is an excellent tour for skiers of all abilities. However, when it is icy only skiers with advanced basic skills should attempt it.

The Flying Loop (named for the most common mode of descent) is the most challenging of the three trails. The first ¾ mile of the loop is skied in conjunction with the Squirrel Run Trail. Once the two trails part there is a 1½-mile climb to the ridge top, where you ski ½ mile along the crest before plunging back down. The final mile of the loop rejoins the Squirrel Run Trail for the descent back to the Sno-Park. When the snow is soft, this 5-mile trail is skiable by anyone with intermediate-level skills. When the snow is icy, skip this loop entirely.

70 FISH LAKE VIEW

Skill level: intermediate
Round trip: 5 miles
Skiing time: 3 hours
Elevation gain: 900 feet
High point: 3000 feet

Best: mid-December–March
Avalanche potential: moderate
Map: Green Trails, Plain

See map on page 184.

Celebrate. This tour follows one of the few skiable roads in the Chiwawa River area that is not usurped by snowmobiles. The objective of the tour is a viewpoint on Pole Ridge high above frozen Fish Lake, reached via a steep forest road. In fact, the road is so steep it is only skiable after a snowstorm covers it with at least 6 inches of new powder snow.

Access: Drive Highway 2 east 19 miles from Steven Pass and turn left on Highway 207 for 4.6 miles. Pass the south entrance to Lake Wenatchee State Park, cross the Wenatchee River, and go right on County Road 22, signed "Chiwawa Loop Road." In 1 mile go left on the Chiwawa River Road. In 2.3 miles find Forest Road 6300 (2100 feet). There are several small Sno-Park areas nearby. If these are full or unplowed, go back .2 mile to a larger Sno-Park on the East Fish Lake Road.

The Tour: The first mile follows an almost level, groomed snowmobile expressway. Pass several groomed spur roads headed for either the Chiwawa River on the right or Fish Lake on the left. Near 1 mile, at a bend in the road, find Road (6300)131 on the left and start climbing steeply. At approximately ½ mile pass a spur road on the right. At 1½ miles (2½ miles from the car), reach the viewpoint (3000 feet).

Fish Lake is directly below and Lake Wenatchee a bit farther away. On the horizon are the snowy peaks of the Stewart Range, Big Jim Mountain, and the Chiwaukum Range. Behind Lake Wenatchee are the steep cliffs of Nason Ridge. On a nice weekend, look for ice fishermen, tiny black dots on the frozen lake. The high whining sound of snowmobiles is everywhere, whether they are in view or not. The road goes on, and in a ¼ mile reaches a slightly higher viewpoint. The road then makes a mile-long, easy descending traverse to a switchback and more downhill to a dead end.

In a region teeming with snowmobiles, it would be nice if the Forest Service could reserve a road just for skiers. How about this one? Or how about this one and maybe one more? There are nearly 80 miles of roads in the Chiwawa River–Fish Lake area groomed for snowmobiles; setting aside 20 untouched miles of roads for skiers would not be excessive.

Let the Forest Service know what roads you would like to have set aside for self-propelled winter recreation by writing to the District Ranger of the Lake Wenatchee Ranger District, Star Route, Box 109, Leavenworth, Washington 98826.

Fish Lake, Lake Wenatchee, Nason Ridge and the Chiwaukum Mountains

71 WHITE RIVER VIEWPOINT

Skill level: advanced basic
Round trip: 10 miles
Skiing time: 6 hours
Elevation gain: 900 feet

High point: 2880 feet
Best: January–February
Avalanche potential: none
Map: Green Trails, Lake Wenatchee

From a vantage point atop sheer cliffs on the side of Dirtyface Peak, look out over the meandering Little Wenatchee River as it enters Lake Wenatchee, then up to formidable Nason Ridge in its warlike armor of snow, Wenatchee Ridge to the west, and the scholarly Poet Peaks beyond. On the way to and from the viewpoint, Glacier Peak puts the finishing touch on the northern horizon.

Nason Ridge from the White River Viewpoint

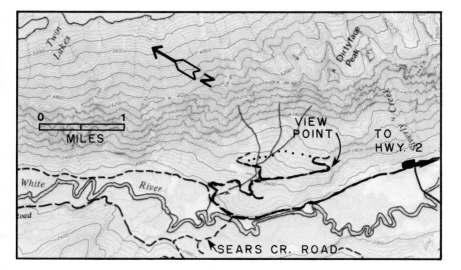

The vantage point is the highlight of a 5-mile ski. The first 3 miles along the White River road are nearly level and skiable by all skill levels. The final 2 miles are up a well-maintained logging road, best for skiers with some experience. On the return trip advanced skiers may make a cross-country loop through heavy timber, a challenge not only to skiing but to routefinding ability.

Access: Drive Highway 2 east from Stevens Pass 19 miles and turn left toward Lake Wenatchee on Road 207. Pass Lake Wenatchee State Park and the road to Plain, and another to Fish Lake. At 13.5 miles from Highway 2 turn right on the White River Road. Park in .2 mile at the end of the plowed road (1920 feet).

The Tour: The White River Road tends to be rutted and often icy. It receives considerable snowmobile use by homeowners in addition to recreationists. The Forest Service, in an attempt to minimize ski-snowmobile conflicts, requests skiers to stay on the south (left) side of the road and snowmobilers to stay on the north (right) side. On your way back you should be able to ski in your own tracks, untrammelled by snowmobiles.

The ski up the valley is beautiful, bounded by the steep flanks of 6240-foot Dirtyface Peak and Wenatchee Ridge. At 3 miles, ¼ mile past the Sears Creek cutoff, turn right and head uphill, following the viewpoint signs. At the top of a large clearcut take a breather and gaze up the White River toward 7420-foot Mount David, with Glacier Peak beyond. Pass two partially overgrown spur roads, the first on the right and the second on the left, to reach the viewpoint at 5 miles (2880 feet). To the south Round Mountain, Alpine, and Mount Mastiff are strung together by Nason Ridge. To the west are the patchy clearcuts on Wenatchee Ridge. Below are flat plains where the Little Wenatchee and White rivers flow into Lake Wenatchee. Unless you have 8-foot skis stay back from the edge—it's a long ski jump to the bottom.

A short loop may be made by continuing up past the viewpoint. The road, partially overgrown from here on, ends in ½ mile. From there head off left through the trees, descending north along a series of benches to reach a deep gully. Cross to the other side and follow the gully (with creek, if flowing) down to intersect the second of the two spur roads passed on the way up. Ski down the spur to the viewpoint road to close the 2-mile loop.

72 LITTLE WENATCHEE RIVER ROAD

Skill level: basic
Round trip: 5 miles
Skiing time: 2 hours
Elevation gain: none

High point: 1960 feet
Best: January–February
Avalanche potential: none
Map: Green Trails, Wenatchee Lake

The Little Wenatchee River Road has ideal terrain for first-time skiers and family groups. The road is virtually flat, which will please the novices, and it is scenic, which will please the more experienced. There is a small meadow right at the start to take those first strides in, and small hills for children to zoom down with cries of "Watch me!"

Access: Drive Highway 2 east 19 miles from Stevens Pass and turn left at Coles Corner on Highway 207. Head north 10.9 miles around Lake Wenatchee. At the north end of the lake go left on the Little Wenatchee River road No. 6500 and drive 1½ miles to a gate. Park in the space provided (1960 feet).

The Tour: Before heading out on your tour, use the meadow on the south side of the road for a few practice strides, glides, and stops. When you feel that everyone is balanced on their skis, head up the road.

The Little Wenatchee River Road tunnels its way through the forest along the base of Wenatchee Ridge. At the end of the first mile the river swings over to the north side of the valley and there are views over the open river channel south to Nason Ridge and west to Mount Mastiff.

The river swings back to the south side of the valley near 2¼ miles and spur road 6502 branches off to the right ¼ mile beyond, marking a good turnaround point for groups with novice skiers.

Skiers continuing on will find the Little Wenatchee River Road remains nearly level until it divides 2¼ miles farther up the valley. Go left at this junction to reach Riverside Campground in ⅛ mile.

Little Wenatchee River Road and Nason Ridge

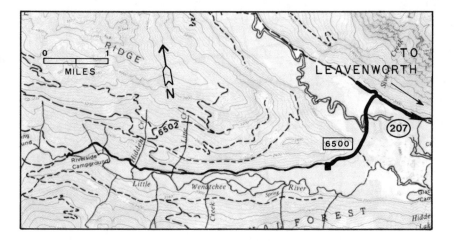

73 WENATCHEE RIVER WAY

Skill level: basic
Round trip: 8 miles to powerlines
Skiing time: 4 hours
Elevation gain: 413 feet

High point: 2000 feet
Best: January–February
Avalanche potential: low
Map: Green Trails, Leavenworth

The Wenatchee River Way is an "over hill, over dale" type of ski tour on a narrow country road. The route takes you through forests, past

Paralleling the Wenatchee River on Wenatchee River Way

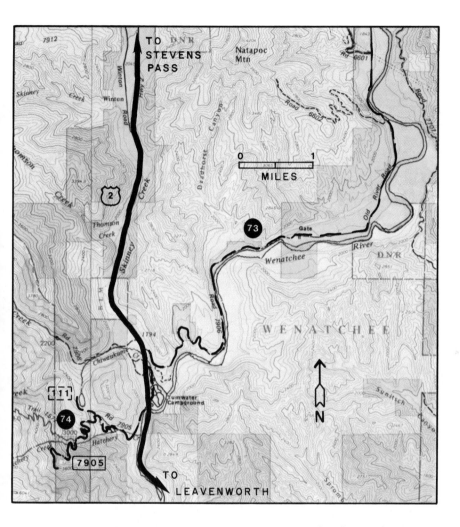

farms, across hills, and along the banks of the Wenatchee River. The one
major problem of the tour involves getting across Chiwaukum Creek to
the start of the Wenatchee River Road—you'll need to take a short walk
across a bridge on Highway 2. The happy result of this access problem is
that few snowmobiles find their way onto this secluded corridor along
the river.

Access: Drive Highway 2 east 26.8 miles from Stevens Pass to the Tumwater Campground entrance (1687 feet). Park in the large turnout on the
east side of the highway.

The Tour: Ski into the campground, then take one of the loop roads
heading north, away from the Wenatchee River, past snow-covered

193

campsites closely paralleling Highway 2. In about ½ mile the way is blocked by brush. Ski up left to the highway and walk across the Chiwaukum Creek Bridge. Get off the highway as soon as possible and ski along the bank until you intercept the Wenatchee River Road to the right.

The Wenatchee River Road starts off in an open meadow, bends to the right, then heads uphill into the forest. Spur roads on the right lead to a future housing development. With more ups than downs, the Wenatchee River Road climbs to a high point about 400 feet above the river at 1½ miles from the campground. Pass a large sandstone outcropping before starting a lazy descent toward the river.

At 2 miles ski along the road as it passes between a house and a barn, then reenters the woods. At about 2½ miles the road reaches the river-bank and stays more or less at water level for the rest of the way to the powerlines and a plowed road from the town of Plain.

The road runs through a narrow band of land between the forested hill-side and the river. Several small campsites are passed right along the edge of the river. If camping, plan on melting snow for water—do not drink the river water.

74 HATCHERY CREEK

Skill level: intermediate
Round trip: 5 miles
Skiing time: 3 hours
Elevation gain: 1100 feet
High point: 2800 feet
Best: mid-December–March

Avalanche potential: moderate
Maps: Green Trails, Leavenworth
and Chiwaukum Mtns.

See map on page 193.

This tour starts at the edge of Tumwater Canyon where the hillsides rise straight to the sky, blocking out the sun for most of the short winter days. You'll ski high up the outer slopes of the Chiwaukum Mountains above Tumwater Canyon to a viewpoint overlooking the Tumwater Range or to a small hidden lake nestled in the steep hills. The upper section of the trip receives considerably more sunlight and warmth than the shady start, so if you are waxing your skies be prepared for everything from powdery snow at the bottom to slush at the top.

Access: Drive Highway 2 to the west side of the bridge over the Wenatchee River. Find Hatchery Creek road No. 7905 just 300 feet west of

Hatchery Creek Road

the Forest Service's Tumwater Campground. A small parking area is usually plowed near the bridge and at the entrance to the campground (1687 feet).

The Tour: Ski the forest road along the river, past several summer cottages, and then uphill through a long series of switchbacks. At 1¼ miles is an unmarked junction; stay right. At 2 miles the road gains a 2200-foot saddle between a rounded knob and the clearcut slopes of the main hill. A spur road on the right, Road (7905)111, climbs gently for ½ mile to a small unnamed lake at 2380 feet.

Skiers in search of views should bypass the lake and continue the switchback ascent up sparsely wooded slopes. At 2¼ miles, stay right at another unmarked junction. At approximately 2½ miles the Lake Augusta trailhead parking area is reached, an excellent protected campsite (2800 feet). The road continues on a short distance past the trailhead, then becomes a cat track, ending in steep clearcuts overlooking the Wenatchee River Valley and the rolling hills beyond.

Avoid this upper road after extremely heavy snowfalls. While avalanche hazard is almost zilch for most of the winter, after heavy snows the steep logging clearings of the upper end of the road sometimes cut loose. At such times forgo the open spaces for the safety of that small unnamed lake, located on spur road (7905)111.

75 LEAVENWORTH

Skill level: basic
10 miles of groomed trails
Skiing time: 1–2 days
Elevation gain: 200 feet

High point: average elevation 1200 feet
Best: January–February
Avalanche potential: none
Map: Green Trails, Leavenworth

Ski beautifully groomed tracks over open fields, skim along banks of the Wenatchee River, or roller-coaster up and down through ponderosa pine forest at the base of Tumwater Mountain—all in the countryside around the town of Leavenworth.

An active cross-country ski club in Leavenworth keeps three trails groomed; a small donation is asked to help keep the grooming machines running. Skiers of all levels find appropriate challenges in the set tracks: beginners find them as asset in keeping the boards going in the right direction; intermediates practice technique without worrying about becoming lost or having the encumbrance of a pack; advanced skiers work on stride and ski for time.

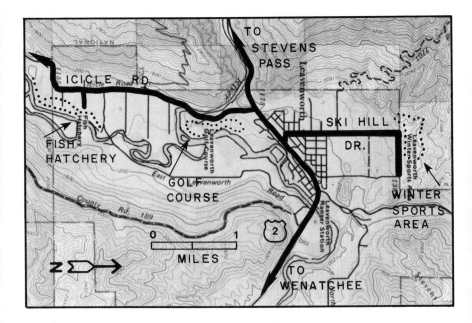

Paralleling the Wenatchee River on the Golf Course loops

Golf Course: The most popular area is the golf course. At the west edge of Leavenworth turn south off Highway 2 on Icicle Road. Drive .6 mile to the Golf Course Road and turn left on it .1 mile to the end.

There are two loops. The outer loop, most suitable for beginners, circles the course in about 2 miles. The inner loop is about 1 mile longer and requires good control on the hills.

Fish Hatchery: Drive 2.1 miles on Icicle Road, then turn left on Hatchery Road for .3 mile to the hatchery. Park in front of the main buildings and walk to the road-end.

Ski trails—only occasionally groomed—head south along the levee on the hatchery side of Icicle Creek and circle through forest, fields, and a housing development. The terrain is mostly level, good for families.

Leavenworth Ski Hill: Near the west end of town turn north on Ski Hill Drive for 1.4 miles up through orchards to the winter sports area. Just inside the gate starts a 1½-mile, regularly groomed loop. This is the most challenging of the three trails, going up and down and winding around the rolling hills.

The Wenatchee River seen from the ski trails in Leavenworth

76 LAKE STUART

Skill level: mountaineer
Round trip: 17 miles
Skiing time: 2 days
Elevation gain: 3064 feet
High point: 5064 feet

Best: April–mid-May
Avalanche potential: high
Maps: Green Trails, Chiwaukum
  Mtns. and Mount Stuart

The tour to this scenic lake nestled under the imposing north face of Mount Stuart provides a challenging backcountry trip with tremendous scenery and, if the timing is right, excellent skiing. This is a mountaineering trip, not because the skiing is difficult but because you'll need competent map-reading skills and the ability to assess the avalanche conditions.

April, when the road is open to within a couple of miles of the trailhead, is generally the best time for this trip. Go when Icicle Creek Road is at least opened as far as Bridge Creek. If uncertain about the road conditions, check with the Forest Service at Leavenworth.

Access: Drive Highway 2 to Leavenworth. At the west end of town turn south on Icicle Creek Road. At 8.5 miles turn left on Road 7601, pass

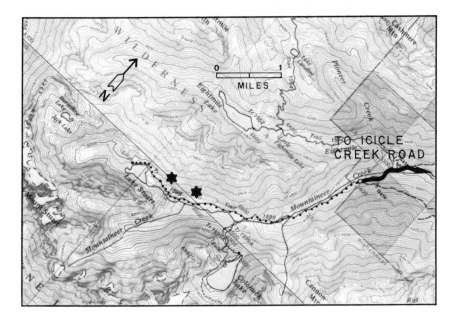

Lake Stuart and Mount Stuart

through Bridge Creek Campground, and cross Icicle Creek (2000 feet). Tour mileages are noted from the bridge; any extra distance driven is a bonus.

The Tour: Ski or hike up Road 7601, passing the Eightmile Trail at 3 miles to reach Mountaineer Creek Trailhead at an abrupt bend in the road at 4 miles (3540 feet).

The trail starts through thick timber paralleling Mountaineer Creek and soon enters the Alpine Lakes Wilderness. The confining wall of trees makes the trail easy to follow for the first mile. Near ¾ mile the trail cuts a steep slope with a direct drop to the creek below. Avoid this short section by cutting up to the top of the terrace directly above. Five miles from Icicle Creek Road (3920 feet) the trail crosses Mountaineer Creek on a broad bridge. Use considerable caution here—no guardrails to keep the careless from a cold bath.

The next mile is spent climbing steeply, with an occasional switchback, past giant boulders and over rock shelves. Expect to walk in this section if the snowmelt is well advanced. The trail divides at 6½ miles (4600 feet). The left fork follows the East Fork Mountaineer Creek to Colchuck Lake, while the right fork enters a broad marshy valley and continues on toward Lake Stuart. Use caution in this area, as there are several avalanche chutes above you during the next mile.

In the final mile to the lake, the trail veers west away from Mountaineer Creek into the Lake Stuart drainage. Switchback up a steep hillside, then follow a narrow band of timber, staying well to the right of the creek, to reach the 5064-foot lake, 8½ miles from Icicle Creek. Set up camp in the protected forest areas near either the outlet or the inlet of the lake. Then settle back to enjoy the view.

Beautiful telemarking slopes above the lake beckon. The least avalanche-prone and largest bowls are northwest of Lake Stuart toward Jack Ridge or Horseshoe and Jack lakes. There you will encounter postcard views of Mount Stuart and Ingalls Peak.

MISSION RIDGE

77 PIPELINE SKI TRAIL

Skill level: basic
Round trip: 5 miles
Skiing time: 2 hours
Elevation gain: 120 feet

High point: 4920 feet
Best: January–February
Avalanche potential: none
Map: USGS, Mission Peak

For those of you who are not surfers, the Banzai Pipeline is a wave that breaks over a coral reef in Hawaii. As the water covering the reef is only three feet deep, the wave has the reputation of doing to surfers what a shredder does to paper. Naturally surfers come from all around the world for the honor of taking a tumble there.

The pipeline in this tour is about as different from the Banzai Pipeline as you can get. It is wide and level for almost its entire distance and it is an excellent place for beginners to try out their skis for the very first time.

Access: Drive to Wenatchee and follow the signs to Mission Ridge Ski Area. Park with the downhill skiers (4800 feet).

The Tour: The tour begins behind the lodge and follows the cat track uphill. The cat track starts out heading north, then switchbacks south, paralleling the ski lift. This is the only hazardous section of the entire tour, as the cat track is shared with banzai beginner downhill skiers. Keep to the far edge of the track and stay single file through this section. (You may avoid this section by buying a ticket and riding the first lift up to the top of the cat track.)

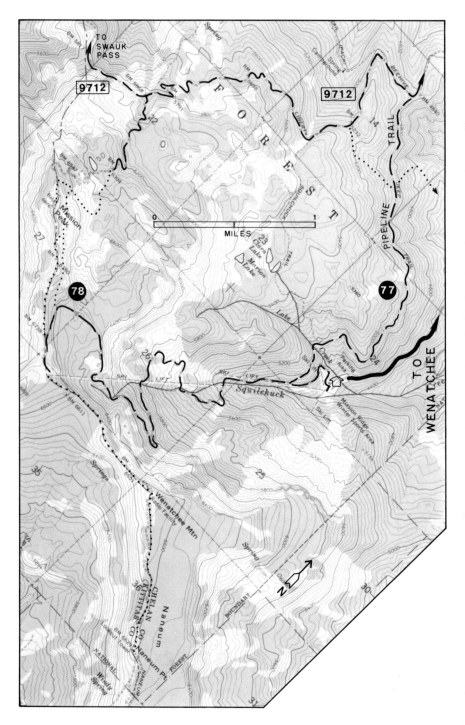

Forest Road 7121

Climb the cat track for ½ mile then watch on your right for a weathered wooden sign noting the start of the Pipeline Ski Trail. The trail heads north, descending about 120 feet in the next 2 miles. Once on the pipeline, the route is obvious and you may settle back to enjoy the tour.

Near the 1½-mile mark the Pipeline Trail is crossed by another ski trail marked in blue diamonds. This intermediate-level trail starts from the end of Forest Road 7121 and climbs steeply through dense timber, crosses the Pipeline Trail, then switchbacks up to Road 9712.

The Pipeline Trail ends at the Liberty-Beehive road No. 9712. This road is a popular snowmobile route and not very appealing to skiers. However, for those who wish to continue, there is an easy-to-ski trail that starts at the end of the Pipeline Trail, right on the other side of Road 9712. This trail follows Road (9712)240 for 1 mile along the crest of a ridge.

Skiers looking for views or a scenic spot for a picnic should climb the steep knoll to the right at the end of the Pipeline Trail. Once on top there are sandstone pillars to explore as well as the endless rolling hills to gaze over.

Mount Rainier from Mission Ridge

78 MISSION RIDGE

Naneum Point

Skill level: intermediate
Round trip: 8 miles
Skiing time: 4 hours
Elevation gain: 400 feet
High point: 6747 feet
Best: January–mid-February
Avalanche potential: none
Map: USGS, Mission Peak

Mission Peak

Skill level: intermediate
Round trip: 8 miles
Skiing time: 5 hours
Elevation gain: 300 feet
High point: 6884 feet
Best: January–February
Avalanche potential: low
Map: USGS, Mission Peak

See map on page 202.

A chairlift ticket is the key to two outstanding backcountry tours along the crest of Mission Ridge. One tour heads east from the chairlift across the rounded ridge crest to views, superb touring, and excellent telemark slopes, ending at the lookout tower on Naneum Point. The second tour heads west from the chairlift, skirting the ragged ridge top to Mission Peak. There are endless views, outstanding telemark slopes, and good touring the entire distance.

Access: Drive to Wenatchee and follow the signs to Mission Ridge Ski Area. Buy a one-way chairlift ticket, which allows you to ride the two chairs needed to reach the top of Mission Ridge (6740 feet).

Naneum Point: From the chairlift terminal at the summit of Mission Ridge, ski left (east) along the ridge crest, following the downhill skiers' trail. The trail soon divides; take either the right or left fork (the right is the easiest) and ski along the ridge to a saddle. Continue east, still following the downhill skiers' tracks.

Ski past the ski-area boundary at ½ mile and climb up a long open hill to the radio facility on Wenatchee Mountain (6742 feet). The view here, as along the entire ridge, is outstanding. Mount Adams lies to the southwest and Glacier Peak and the Columbia River to the north. For telemarking, try the slopes southwest of the peak.

The ridge now turns southeast, descending gradually. Stay to the west side of the broad ridge crest to reach the lookout tower 2 miles from the chairlift.

To return to your car, ski back to the chairlift, where you have your pick of the downhill runs. The easiest run heads west along the ridge crest from the lift and descends 4 miles along a well-graded cat track to the lodge.

Mission Peak: From the chairlift, ski right (west) along the crest of the ridge on a cat track. Pass the radio relay station and head down through the trees to a lightly forested basin (6560 feet). Leave the cat track here and head left (west) up through the basin, skirting along the base of the north side of Mission Ridge. (An alternate method is to ski the crest of the ridge. Leave the ridge after 1 mile at the base of Mission Peak.)

Mission Ridge ends at the rock-bound summit of Mission Peak. To reach the summit, ski to the northwest end of the peak and follow the ridge back (6876 feet). The best skiing is found on the open slopes north of the peak.

To return to your car, ski northeast from the peak, down into a sloping basin. Descend north out of the base of the basin following a ski route marked with blue diamonds. At the lower end of the basin (6300 feet) ski into the forest on a narrow logging road and continue the descent to Road 9712 (5868 feet). Turn right and ski the road as it winds through two open meadows, climbs for ½ mile, then descends steeply. On the way down you will pass the Clare Lake Trail, several marked ski trails, and the Devils Gulch Trail.

At 6 miles from the chairlift go right on the Pipeline Ski Trail (see Tour 77). Ski south for 2 level miles back to the ski area, where you will turn left to descend the cat track back to the parking lot.

79 MISSION RIDGE TO SWAUK PASS TRAVERSE

Skill level: intermediate
Round trip: 19 miles or 24 miles
Skiing time: 2 days
Elevation gain: 1000 feet
High point: 6720 feet

Best: January–mid-March
Avalanche potential: moderate
Maps: USGS, Mission Peak and
*   Liberty*

Skiing from Mission Ridge to Swauk Pass makes a superb traverse of the Wenatchee Mountains. The traverse starts from a high point on Mission Ridge, then heads northwest past Mission Peak and follows the

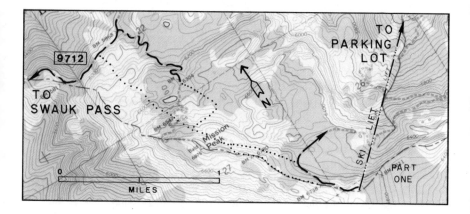

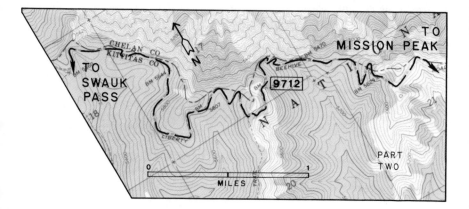

winding course of a rolling ridge crest to Haney Meadows, where there is a choice of road or trail for the descent to Swauk Pass.

Neither the skiing nor the routefinding on this traverse is difficult, the route being mostly on logging roads packed solid by snowmobile use. The scenery is excellent and there are plenty of opportunities to drop your pack and take a run down open slopes. There are campsites along the entire traverse. Plan to melt snow for water.

Access: Leave one car at the summit of Swauk Pass in the Sno-Park on the south side of Highway 97. Then drive north to Highway 2 and follow it east to Wenatchee, where you follow the signs to Mission Ridge Ski Area. Let the parking attendants know you will be leaving your car overnight. (If there are no attendants, check in at the ski-area office or the ski-patrol office.)

The Tour: Buy a one-way skier's ticket to the summit of Mission Ridge. Start your trip to the top by riding the chair nearest to the lodge. From the top of the first chair, ski left down a short hill to the start of the chair that will carry you and your pack to the summit of the ridge (6720 feet).

From the top of the upper chair, ski right (west) along the ridge top. First take in views that include Mount Adams, Mount Rainier, Mount Stuart, and Glacier Peak, then ski along the cat track past a radio relay building and down into a forested basin. Leave the cat track at ½ mile when it bends right (6560 feet) and ski uphill to the northwest. Keeping Mission Ridge to your left, ski along its base to Mission Peak. Here you may either follow the ridgeline north, keeping to the right of the crest to Forest Road 9712 (5820 feet), or head northeast into a sloping basin and

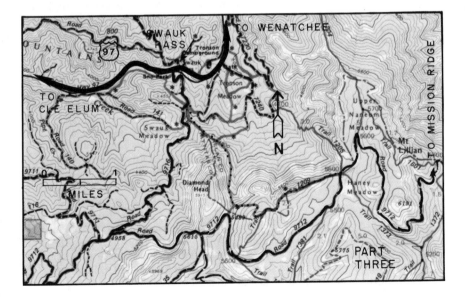

Mission Peak

follow a ski trail marked by blue diamonds north. At the north end of the basin is a jeep road which descends to Road 9712 at 2½ miles from the chairlift.

Once on Road 9712 the route is straightforward. Go left (northwest) and follow the road along the ridge, sometimes to the right of the crest, sometimes to the left. At 7 miles from the chairlift the road bends south, climbs over a 5900-foot summit, then divides. The left fork follows a ridge south to Grouse Springs; ignore it. Stay on the right fork (Road 9712).

At 9½ miles the road skirts the edge of steep sandstone cliffs. Do not ski too close to the north side of the ridge in this area. One mile farther, the road bends south around Mount Lillian. Upper Naneum Meadow are reached at 13½ miles. (A very scenic campsite may be found 1 mile north of the road at the upper end of the meadows overlooking the Swauk Pass Highway and the Mount Stuart Range).

At 14 miles the Tronsen Meadow Trail is passed on the right and ¼ mile beyond, also on the right, is the ski trail to Swauk Pass. This 5-mile trail is well marked with blue diamonds, all intersections are signed, and reaches the pass at the 19-mile mark. However, the trail is narrow and steep in sections and crosses an avalanche path. This trail is unpleasant when the snow is icy or has a breakable crust, and dangerous after a heavy snowfall.

Road 9712 passes a small wooden cabin on the edge of Haney Meadow at 14½ miles (open to the public and generally occupied in the winter), then heads west for 4 level miles to the Table Mountain intersection. Continue straight for 2 more miles, then turn right on Road 9716 and descend north to reach Swauk Pass 24 miles from the start.

80 CAMAS LAND

Skill level: advanced basic
Round trip: 4 miles
Skiing time: 2 hours
Elevation gain: 550 feet

High point: 3450 feet
Best: mid-December–February
Avalanche potential: low
Map: Green Trails, Liberty

Meadows keynote this tour, which starts at Camas Land (a 2-mile-long meadow), then climbs past several smaller meadows and marshes before the trip ends at a breathtaking viewpoint.

Now the bad news—the access to the area is often more of a challenge than the tour. If you do not drive a truck or a four-wheel-drive, be sure and carry tire chains for the final section of the Camas Creek Road.

Access: Drive Highway 97 south 4.4 miles from Highway 2, then turn left (east) on Camas Creek Road No. 7200. If coming from the south, the Camas Creek Road is 16.2 miles north of Swauk Pass Summit. Once on Camas Creek Road, drive 2.2 miles up to Camas Land, where the road divides. Stay right and follow the road as it skirts around the west side of the meadow for another .5 mile. The road will climb a short, steep hill, then level off. When the plowed road turns east, branching off from Camas Creek Road, park (2900 feet).

The Tour: Ski up Forest Road 7200 (Camas Creek Road), climbing gently

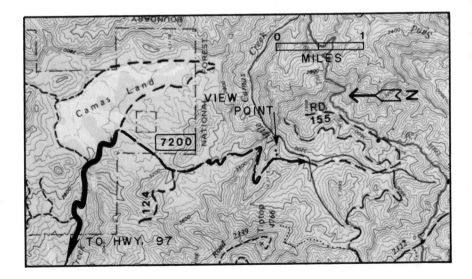

along the east side of the open valley. On your right is a wide meadow, crisscrossed by small creeks, coyote trails, ski tracks, and snowmobile ruts. This is a great place to explore after a snowfall when the meadow is fresh.

Road 7200 is groomed for snowmobiles, so be ready to jump out of the way whenever a pack of machines zips by. However, for the most part this is a quiet tour as it passes from meadow into the forest. At ¾ mile pass spur road (7200)124 on the right. (This road contours 1½ miles west before ending and is not nearly as scenic as what is to come.)

At 1½ miles Road 7200 levels off for ¼ mile, then climbs steeply over a shoulder of Tip Top Mountain to reach the viewpoint. Go left for the best views, being careful to stay well away from the overhung left-hand side of the ridge. Directly below on the left is a series of weathered sandstone pinnacles and ribs. Beyond is a wall of strikingly beautiful white sandstone. To the east lies Burch Mountain, to the south are the Wenatchee Mountains, and to the west is the summit of Tip Top Mountain.

For those of you who wish to continue on, there are miles and miles of logging roads to ski. However, beyond the viewpoint, Road 7200 makes two long descents, passing two meadows in the next 1½ miles before it ends. The tour then continues on spur road (7200)155, which climbs up to the ridge tops before it ends at 3988 feet.

Note: Camas Land is private property and not open to the public. Follow the tour as described above and you will be on public land, open for touring. If you wish to do some further exploring, go 100 feet west from the start of this tour and ski up a gated forest road that is closed to snowmobiles. This road is ½ mile long and ends at a seed farm.

Horse Lake Mountain from viewpoint

Miller Peak from Ruby Creek Road

81 RUBY CREEK

Skill level: advanced basic
Round trip: 4 miles or more
Skiing time: 2 hours or more
Elevation gain: 1000 feet

High point: 3000 feet
Best: December–March
Avalanche potential: moderate
Map: Green Trails, Liberty

Need some fun and exercise but still want to get home in time to watch the Seahawks? Then this tour might be the ticket. The Ruby Creek Road traverses the hillside high above the valley floor, wandering in and out of narrow side canyons. Longer tours on the side roads, which descend down to Ruby Creek and climb to views on the far side, are also suggested.

This tour is another one of those yo-yos that vary with the snowline. Be sure to carry an up-to-date Forest Service road map as well as a contour map to plan your tour according to the snow level.

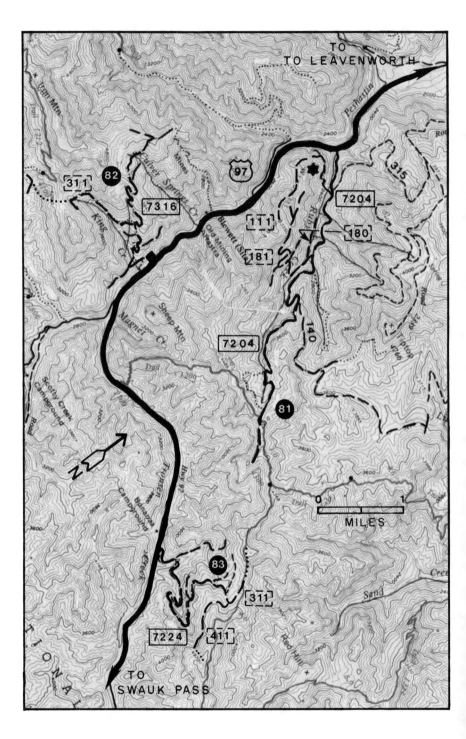

Access: Drive Highway 97 south 9.1 miles from Highway 2 and turn left on Ruby Creek road No. 7204, (2000 feet). Typically there is only enough space for three cars or one truck and snowmobile trailer, so leave as much parking room as possible for your fellow skiers. If approaching from the south, Ruby Creek Road is located 12.5 miles north of Swauk Pass on the east side of Highway 97.

The Tour: Ruby Creek Road starts in a narrow canyon with towering rock walls that gradually open up as the road climbs away from Highway 97. Skiing in this section is scenic, but watch for snow and rock sloughing off from the steep hillsides.

After ½ mile you'll encounter two spur roads. The first is on the right, Road (7201)315, heading to Tiptop Lookout Site, some 7 miles above. The second is spur road (7204)111, heading down to cross Ruby Creek then up to excellent views on Windmill Point, a possible destination only when the snow pack is stable (avalanche hazard exists on the long, open traverse to Windmill Point after any snowfall).

After 1 mile of the road up Ruby Creek levels off and begins winding through the first of two deep side canyons. At 1¾ miles comes a second chance to reach Windmill Point; this is a considerably safer approach. To reach the point, ski right and down across Ruby Creek on spur road 180, then climb up the opposite side of the valley, where both spur 181 gives views out to the Stuart Range.

If the snow has melted high up Ruby Creek or you're feeling energized, it is 6½ miles up the Ruby Creek Road to road's end at a high and scenic overlook (4350 feet). And if your bionic legs still haven't had enough, go back to spur road (7200)140 and ski for uncountable miles over to upper Camas Creek and on and on and on.

Tracks of a snowshoe hare

82 KING CREEK ROAD

Skill level: intermediate
Round trip: 8 miles
Skiing time: 4 hours
Elevation gain: 2000 feet
High point: 4440 feet

Best: January–mid-March
Avalanche potential: moderate
Map: Green Trails, Liberty

See map on page 212.

Views, excellent powder bowls, and early-season corn snow all combine to make King Creek Road an outstanding tour.

Although the road is closed in the summer to motorized traffic, during the winter months snowmobiles are allowed. Fortunately, there are better

The Stuart Range from the end of King Creek Road

roads for snowmobiles close by and King Creek is largely ignored by the motorized crowd.

Access: Drive Highway 97 south 12 miles from Highway 2 or north from Swauk Pass for 9.5 miles. There is a small parking area on the west side of the highway at the start of King Creek road No. 7316, (2440 feet).

The Tour: The road heads south on a section of the old Blewett Pass Road, paralleling Highway 97 while it crosses Peshastin Creek, passes a miner's cabin, and crosses King Creek, all in the first ⅛ mile.

The climb starts at the first switchback. At the second switchback you will be faced with a gate that must be climbed over or skied around. Beyond this point the road is poorly marked. Numerous minor spur roads branch off, generally unsigned. Near 2800 feet, the first main spur branches left, Road (7316)211.

Continue to climb the open south-facing slope. If confused at intersections, the main road is always the one that switchbacks. Near 2¾ miles, the road swings into a small basin where spur road (7316)311 branches to the left.

The road reaches a 3843-foot vantage point overlooking Peshastin Creek, Sheep Mountain, Tip Top Mountain, and Table Mountain at 3 miles. Here the road divides. The right-hand fork offers an excellent launch pad down to a powder bowl. The main road (No. 7316) follows the left spur for about 50 feet to a second intersection, then turns right for another mile to a ridge overlooking Negro Creek, the Three Brothers, and the Stuart Range.

The Iron Mountain Road can be reached from the King Creek area by skiing down Road 7316 to the 2¾-mile mark, then following Road (7316)311 northwest to the base of a clearing. Ski up to the crest of a saddle at the top of the clearing, then west to the Iron Mountain road No. (7322)400 and delightful views of the Negro Creek Basin.

The Stuart Range from Five Mile Road

PESHASTIN CREEK

83 FIVE MILE ROAD

Skill level: advanced basic
Round trip: 6 miles
Skiing time: 4 hours
Elevation gain: 1120 feet
High point: 4160 feet

Best: January–February
Avalanche potential: moderate
Map: Green Trails, Liberty

See map on page 212.

Viewed from below, Tronsen Ridge seems to remain magically free of snow the entire winter. Complete hillsides on the west side of the ridge are clear of snow the day after a storm. This tour approaches Tronsen Ridge via Five Mile Road, a route offering the best of two worlds—a snow-covered road sheltered from sun and dry hillsides for pleasant lunch sites.

Access: Five Mile Road is located on Highway 97 and may be reached by driving south from Highway 2 for 16.3 miles or north from Swauk Pass for 5.2 miles. There is a small parking area at its start on the east side of the highway (3040 feet).

The Tour: Five Mile Road No. 7224 starts by heading south, paralleling Highway 97. After ⅛ mile the road swings east toward Tronsen Ridge, following a creek into a large basin burned off during the dry summer of 1985. As the road enters the basin, it reaches the first of many unmarked junctions. Take the road to the far right, cross the creek, and climb around a narrow rib into a second basin. The road contours around this clearcut basin, crosses a second creek, and climbs a steep north-facing slope with a long switchback.

At 1¾ miles the road crosses a creek and swings back toward the burn, crossing an open, sunbaked slope. Snow may be thin along here so watch for rocks. At 2¼ miles the road swings into the upper section of the burn and enters an area where the roads are numbered. At 2¾ miles, go right on spur road (7224)311, which climbs directly to Tronsen Ridge and views of Iron Mountain to the west and the rolling summits of the Wenatchee Mountains to the east.

Skiers desiring more views may tackle one of the hills along the ridge. The 4536-foot hill to the north can be approached without difficulty by following the ridge crest. The 4970-foot hill to the south is best reached by branching right off Road (7224)311 onto spur road (7224)411. Ski to the end of the road, then go east, straight up to the top of the ridge. Follow the crest south to the summit ⅛ mile beyond.

AND MORE SKI TOURS

The 83 tours covered by this book barely scratch the surface of the skiing opportunities in the North Cascades. The following is a list of other places to explore. Unless otherwise noted, these trails are suggested for advanced basic or intermediate skiers.

Nooksack River

Lookout Mountain Road: Starts from the southwest end of Glacier and climbs high up the hillside toward Lookout Mountain. This road is on private timber-company land.

West Church Ridge Road No. 3120: Starts out steeply, then levels out higher up. Tour begins at the Canyon Creek Road (see Tour 3).

Baker River

Forest Road 12: The upper end of this road is closed to motorized use for much of the winter. See Tour 11 for directions.

Mount Baker via Easton Glacier: Mountaineer tour to the summit of Mount Baker. This is the most straightforward tour up the mountain. Ski to Park Butte (see Tour 11) and continue up to the summit. Some snowmobile use as far up as Sherman Crater.

Koma Kulshan Loop Trail: Practice area for basic-level skiers. Access is from the Baker Lake Road. Park at Nature Trail Sno-Park (see Tour 13) and walk back ½ mile to the ski trail.

Sandy Creek Road No. 1124: Up to 14 miles round trip. Good views from clearcuts and on spur road 1127. Access from Baker Lake Road. Some snowmobile use.

Skagit River

Cascade River Road: Moderate avalanche potential on this 22-mile-long valley-bottom road. Access from Marblemount. Drive Cascade River Road to the end of the plowing.

Boston Basin: Mountaineer-level tour with high avalanche hazard in the basin. Ski in the spring only. Access from Marblemount on the Cascade River Road. Hike or ski in via Diamond Mine Road, then follow the trail into the basin.

Methow River

Harts Pass: Accessed by Road 9400 from Mazama. Avalanches close the road all winter; however, in the late spring there are open slopes for telemarking around the pass area.

Boulder Creek Road No. 37: Miles of roads to explore. Considerable snowmobile use. Access from the East Chewack River Road.

Twisp River Road No. 44: Beginner's tour up the Twisp River Valley. This area receives some snowmobile use.

South Fork Gold Creek: From the Sno-Park on Road 4330 you can ski all the way to the ridge tops overlooking Lake Chelan. This area receives some snowmobile use.

Skykomish River

North Fork Skykomish River Road No. 65: Up to 8 miles each way on the road to Jack Pass. Views of Monte Cristo peaks and the North Fork Valley. Access, drive the North Fork Road 9 miles north from Index to end of plowing.

Barclay Lake: A road and trail tour to the lake. Need stable conditions before setting out on 635th Place NE from the town of Baring. Follow Road 6024 4¼ miles to Trail No. 1055. Continue up the trail another 1½ mile to the forested lake.

Beckler River Road No. 65: Easy river-valley tour along the Beckler River to Jack Pass or, when the road is open for the first 5 miles, ski up the Johnson Creek road No. 6520 for excellent ridge-top views of the Monte Cristo peaks. Access, see Tour 59.

Wenatchee Lake

Sears Creek: Over 16 miles of roads, good views and open slopes. Access, see Tour 71.

Natapoc Ridge: Miles or roads to ski with good views of the Entiat Mountains, Wenatchee River Valley, and the farms of Plain. Access from State Route 209 at the north entrance to Plain. Ski up Forest Road 6601.

Leavenworth

Icicle Creek: Miles of valley-bottom skiing. There is moderate avalanche potential after any snowfall. Access, turn south off Highway 2 at west end of Leavenworth and drive Icicle Creek Road to end of plowing.

TRAILS CLASSIFIED BY USE

Multiple Use
1. Glacier Creek
2. Heliotrope Ridge
3. Canyon Creek
4. Wells Creek
5. Twin Lakes Road
6. North Fork Nooksack
11. Park Butte
12. Anderson Butte
13. Martin Lake—Morovitz Loop
15. Finney Creek
16. Sauk Mountain
17. Oakes Creek
18. Cutthroat Creek
19. Klipchuck—North Cascades Highway
23. Lewis Butte
24. Methow Valley View
26. Buck Mountain Loop
27. Buck Lake
28. Flat Campground and Paul Mountain
29. Doe Mountain
30. Blue Buck Mountain
31. Pipestone Canyon
35. Telemark Mountain
36. Buck Mountain Lookout
37. Smith Canyon
38. Elderberry Canyon
39. Cooper Loops
40. Antilon Lakes
41. Goff Peak
44. White Chuck Mountain View
45. Rat Trap Pass
47. North Mountain
48. Segelsen Creek Road
50. Schweitzer Creek Loop
51. Mallardy Ridge
52. Red Bridge Tour
55. Coal Lake
56. Big Four Loop
57. Lake Elizabeth
59. Eagle Creek
61. Beckler Peak Road
64. Smith Brook and Lake Valhalla
65. Mill Creek
66. Coulter Ski Trail
70. Fish Lake View
71. White River Viewpoint
72. Little Wenatchee River Road
73. Wenatchee River Way
74. Hatchery Creek
78. Mission Ridge
79. Mission Ridge to Swauk Pass Traverse
80. Camas Land
81. Ruby Creek
82. King Creek Road
83. Five Mile Road

Self-Propelled
7. Silver Fir
8. White Salmon Creek
9. Artist Point and Coleman Pinnacle
10. Herman Saddle
14. Mount Shuksan
43. Green Mountain
46. Kennedy Hot Springs
49. Pilchuck Mountain
53. Deer Creek Road
54. Double Eagle Tour
58. Miller River
60. Tonga Ridge and Foss River
62. Heather Ridge
63. Josephine Lake
67. Chiwaukum Mountains (Scottish Lakes)
69. Chiwawa Sno-Park

Groomed Ski Trail
20. Castle Ranch Loop
21. Rendezvous Pass via Fawn Creek
22. Fawn Peak
25. Rendezvous Pass Hut to Hut
32. Sun Mountain
33. Methow Valley Trail (M.V.T.)
34. Loup-Loup
42. Bear Mountain Ranch
68. Lake Wenatchee State Park
75. Leavenworth

Nonmotorized
76. Lake Stuart
77. Pipeline Ski Trail

SUGGESTED READING

Avalanche Safety

Fraser, Colin. *Avalanches and Snow Safety*. New York: Charles Scribner's Sons, 1978.

LaChappelle, E. R. *The ABC of Avalanche Safety*, 2nd ed. Seattle: The Mountaineers, 1985.

Peters, Ed, ed. *Mountaineering: The Freedom of the Hills*. 4th ed. Seattle: The Mountaineers, 1982.

Enjoying the Outdoors (Proper clothing, ski equipment, winter camping)

Brady, Michael. *Cross-Country Ski Gear*, 2nd ed. Seattle: The Mountaineers, 1988.

Tejada-Flores, Lito. *Backcountry Skiing*. San Francisco: Sierra Club Books, 1981.

Watters, Ron. *Ski Camping*. San Francisco: Chronicle Books, 1979.

How To

Barnett, Steve. *Cross-Country Downhill*. 2nd ed. Seattle: Pacific Search Press, 1979.

Bein, Vic. *Mountain Skiing*. Seattle: The Mountaineers, 1982.

Gillette, Ned, and Dostal, John. *Cross-Country Skiing*. 3rd ed. Seattle: The Mountaineers, 1988.

First Aid

Lentz, Martha; Macdonald, Steven; and Carline, Jan. *Mountaineering First Aid*, 3rd ed. Seattle: The Mountaineers, 1985.

Wilkerson, James A., M.D., ed. *Medicine for Mountaineering*. 3rd ed. Seattle: The Mountaineers, 1985.

INDEX

About the authors:

Tom Kirkendall and Vicky Spring, residents of Edmonds, Washington, are both experienced outdoor people and enthusiastic skiers. The couple travel the hills in summer as hikers, backpackers and cyclists on mountain bikes; when the snow falls, they pin on cross-country skis and keep on exploring. Both Vicky and Tom studied at the Brooks Institute of Photography in Santa Barbara, California, and are now building their careers together as outdoor photographers and guidebook authors. Vicky (who first stood up on skis at age three) had something of a head start in the field, beginning in the days when she carried a backpack of camera gear for her well-known outdoor photographer father, Ira Spring.

Vicky and Tom are the authors of *Bicycling the Pacific Coast,* and *Cross-Country Ski Trails of Washington's Cascades and Olympics;* she is co-author and photographer of *94 Hikes* and *95 Hikes in the Canadian Rockies;* and he is author/photographer of *Mountain Bike Adventures in Washington's North Cascades & Olympics* and *in Washington's South Cascades & Puget Sound,* all published by The Mountaineers.

224

Other books from The Mountaineers include:

CROSS-COUNTRY SKI ROUTES of Oregon's Cascades, Klindt Vielbig
Details and maps on 197 tours, loops and connector links, for skiers from beginning to intermediate, for Mt. Hood, Bend areas.

ABC OF AVALANCHE SAFETY, 2nd ED., Ed LaChapelle
Classic handbook on basics of avalanches — determining potential areas, traveling in avalanche terrain, reactions if caught, search, rescue.

CROSS-COUNTRY SKIING, 3rd Ed., Ned Gillette, John Dostal
Zany and instructive how-to information on skiing everything from track to backcountry, by two experts.

HYPOTHERMIA, FROSTBITE AND OTHER COLD INJURIES: Prevention, Recognition, Prehospital Treatment, Wilkerson, Bangs, Hayward
Medical experts describe hypothermia's effects on the body, how to avoid it, how to recognize signs and how to treat it; includes frostbite and immersion.

SNOWSHOEING, 3rd Ed., Prater
Latest information about equipment and techniques for varying terrain and snow conditions.

Ask for illustrated catalog of more than 200 outdoor titles:

The Mountaineers
1011 S.W. Klickitat Way, Seattle WA 98134
(206) 223-6303
Order toll-free   1-800-553-4453